LEADERSHIP AS SERVICE

LEADERSHIP AS SERVICE

*A New Model for Higher
Education in a New Century*

KENT A. FARNSWORTH

AMERICAN COUNCIL ON EDUCATION
PRAEGER
Series on Higher Education

Library of Congress Cataloging-in-Publication Data

Farnsworth, Kent Allen.
  Leadership as service : a new model for higher education in a new
century / by Kent A. Farnsworth.
      p. cm. — (Ace/praeger series on higher education)
  Includes bibliographical references and index.
  ISBN 0–275–99092–3 (alk. paper)
  1. College administrators—United States.   2. Education, Higher—
United States—Administration.   3. Educational leadership—United
States.   I. Title.
  LB2341.F35 2007
  378.1'11—dc22   2006032831

British Library Cataloguing in Publication Data is available.

Library of Congress Catalog Card Number: 2006032831
ISBN 10: 0–275–99092–3
ISBN 13: 978–0–275–99092–3

First published in 2007

Praeger Publishers, 88 Post Road West, Westport, CT 06881
An imprint of Greenwood Publishing Group, Inc.
www.praeger.com

Printed in the United States of America

The paper used in this book complies with the
Permanent Paper Standard issued by the National
Information Standards Organization (Z39.48–1984).

10   9   8   7   6   5   4   3   2   1

Copyright Acknowledgments

The author and the publisher gratefully acknowledge permission for use of the following:

Lao Tzu's verse from *The Way of Life*, copyright 1944 by Witter Bynner; renewed
© 1972 by Dorothy Chauvenet and Paul Horgan. Reprinted by permission of
HarperCollins Publishers.

Extracts from Ben Shahn, *The Shape of Content*, reprinted by permission of the publisher
from *The Shape of Content* by Ben Shahn, pp. 113-114, Cambridge, Mass.: Harvard
University Press, Copyright © 1957 by the President and Fellows of Harvard College,
renewed 1985 by Bernarda B. Shahn.

Extracts from Arthur Levine, "Worlds Apart: Disconnects Between Students and Their
Colleges," *Declining by Degrees*, eds. Richard H. Hersh and John Merrow (New York:
Palgrave Macmillan) 2005, pp. 158, 164.

This book is dedicated to my father, Dean Farnsworth, for a lifetime of Leadership as Service, and to my mentors in Educational Leadership, Charles McClain, Michael Crawford, and James Tatum.

CONTENTS

PREFACE

For forms of government let fools contest: Whate'er is best administr'd
is best.

—Alexander Pope

When I first learned that I had been selected to preside over a college, a good friend and mentor gave me a copy of James Fisher's *Power of the Presidency,* commenting that, "There is no good preparation for being ultimately responsible—but this can help." I read it carefully and have reread it a number of times since, passing copies along to colleagues who were newly appointed to presidencies. After 19 years in office, I still found Fisher's description of the challenges facing college presidents insightful, and his advice generally sage and useful. During my early years, I was reassured by his observation that my mentor was right—practically no one enters the office with effective preparation for leading an academic institution. Even a deanship or vice presidency has limitations of scope and does not require the delicate interweaving of all institutional and community interests. And, to paraphrase Truman, the buck doesn't stop anywhere else.

Despite this necessary learning curve, Fisher cautioned that there would be an immediate expectation that the new leader should be "effective" on day one. He was right. What we usually refer to as the honeymoon period has become increasingly short and does not include much tolerance for trial and error. Problems, challenges, and opportunities do not wait for the new president to become accustomed to office. They are waiting on the desk when he or she first walks in the door.

That being the case, I found Fisher's list of presidential characteristics that might lead to immediate effectiveness to be useful and on target. Yet in his first chapter, he presented a position concerning the office that I have always found uncomfortable, one that served as a recurring theme throughout this otherwise masterful discussion of presidential leadership. To retain effective power over time, he maintained, the president must develop "an aura of distance and mystery,"[1] and much of what Fisher presented in later chapters was directed at a powerful presidential "image," with what often appeared to be careful manipulation and calculation.

Time in the office taught me that if a president is reasonably effective, the aura and mystique grow without being nurtured, and some accommodation to the aura is healthy, even necessary, for the college. Though the institution I served was relatively small and we worked to foster a 'family' environment among employees, we still encouraged some air of formality, insisting on the use of academic titles when addressing each other on campus, asking that faculty and staff dress in a manner that encouraged respect, and expecting there to be appropriate distance between students, faculty, and professional staff. But in my reading, Fisher occasionally subordinated what was best for others and for the institution to professional expedience, advising presidents to do that which would, in the long run, be best for themselves, for their personal careers, and for longevity in office.

The quote from Pope that begins this Preface is my way of conceding that there is no perfect or flawless approach to leadership or governance, and hundreds of presidents have followed Fisher's thoughtful advice. But I was forced by Fisher and other writers about presidential leadership to ask, "What is my reason for holding office? Am I primarily interested in longevity, or must I be willing, if necessary, to sacrifice tenure in office for some greater achievement?"

I also now see overwhelming evidence that leadership approaches of the past, based upon the bureaucratic, top-down use of power and hierarchical models, are ineffective and occasionally destructive. But so too are laissez-faire, shared governance approaches with no single, responsible chief decision maker. Today's world of rapidly changing technology, explosive growth in information and access to it, and heightened expectations for social equality and global understanding cry out for a new leadership model—leadership based on appreciation for difference and an integrative and power-sharing approach to organizational development. But it also demands that someone be in charge, and be able to move an institution forward as change demands adaptation and occasional reinvention. At the beginning of the 1990s, I began to see evidence that higher education, particularly the pubic sector, would fail altogether in its present form within the next several decades if we were unable to find and introduce new leadership models that better accommodate and direct change, while embracing inclusiveness at the same time.

In my search for that new approach, I found answers partly in a personal philosophy that draws heavily upon religious studies, partly in the thinking of the champions of "new management" such as Peter Drucker, Jim Collins, Stephen Covey, and Warren Bennis, and partly in the work of two revolutionary thinkers about organizations and leadership; Robert Greenleaf and Mary Parker Follett. In combination, these experiences convinced me that leadership, if it is to succeed in the twenty-first century, must ultimately be an act of service and selflessness, combined with a management savvy that keeps service focused and tough-minded. College administration must be a total commitment to the welfare of those being served—commitment to the point of denying personal gain, if necessary.

I am aware that Fisher and others maintain that the mystery, the aura, and mystique strengthen the office, and thereby strengthen the institution and its ability to serve. There may have been a time when this was true, but it has passed. Today's working environment is inclusive rather than exclusive, participatory rather than authoritarian, horizontal rather than hierarchical. Leadership is involving rather than directing—but must be responsible in the sense that we think of this term as meaning "able to respond."

I read Jim Collins's transformational book on organizational effectiveness, *Good to Great*, and its discussion of Level 5 leadership, not with surprise, but as affirmation. He found that those organizations that transcended being "good" and moved on to greatness were most often led by relatively unassuming, credit-sharing, lower profile leaders. They were individuals with a passionate vision of what could be and little concern for who received credit for moving the organization forward. They were servants with savvy.

This book is about educational leadership as service. It argues that when one chooses to be a college leader, one should elect to become professionally selfless. The principle of "service first" should apply to all leadership, and I am constantly disappointed and occasionally disgusted by those who present themselves as so-called public servants, yet use their positions for ego enhancement, personal gain, and exercise of power at the expense of those being served. Even in the private sector where I spent a brief few years, there are compelling arguments, as Collins illustrates, that leadership must become an act of service—to employees, to customers, and to the public environment in which the business operates, rather than strictly to stockholders and the bottom line. The huge and inexcusable abuse of power and trust demonstrated by scandals such as the Enron bankruptcy are cases in point. But my experience is largely limited to education and so, therefore, are most of the observations made in this book.

A colleague once commented that had I spent more time in the down and dirty, rough and tumble world of some of the really tough college leadership situations in the country, I would be more pragmatic about my leadership philosophy. Granted, before moving into a professorial role in the academy, I spent nearly 30 years in administrative roles where boards were thoughtful and responsible, faculty were cooperative and committed, and those leading the institutions tried to model principles of fairness and integrity. In each of these cases—involving three institutional settings in both the university and community college sectors—there were key individuals who believed themselves to be servants first. I am convinced that this commitment *shaped* the environment, rather than served as a coincidental adjunct to it. Absent these key service-oriented leaders, these environments would not have existed as they did. There would have been much greater contention, ethical ambiguity, departmental tribalism, and general selfishness, all of which compromise our sole purpose for being—to contribute through teaching and learning, scholarship and research, to the betterment of the human condition.

Fortunately, in addition to having been nurtured by the mentors just mentioned, my personal sense that leadership is first and foremost an act of service finds support in the writings of some of the newly emerging 'prophets' of leadership's future. I find similar themes in Drucker, Collins, Covey, Bennis, Senge, John Gardner, and others as I read their work. Several decades ago, a friend and colleague, Jim Tatum, introduced me to two earlier pioneers who have become central to shaping my sense of leadership's future. Jim has been something of a giant in the area of college trusteeship. For 40 years, he was one of the most active trustees in the country through his involvement in board training, presidential searches, and trustee leadership. He is a former national board member of the Association of Governing Boards, presided over the Association of Community College Trustees, and was a rare trustee addition to the board of directors of the American Association of Community Colleges. It was through Jim that I became acquainted with the work of Robert Greenleaf and read his seminal essay, "The Servant as Leader." Greenleaf provides much of the underlying philosophical base for the model presented here.

Since becoming a student of Greenleaf, I have felt, however, that his idealism is occasionally too limited to what the leader should be and what the organization should do for its employees, without sufficient discussion of *how*. Greenleaf, as I read him, is long on principle, but short on practice. As a practitioner, I found the few organizational recommendations he does make to be too idealistic, overlooking realities that cannot be ignored in our world of constant change.

Again, through Jim Tatum, I came across the insightful work of the early twentieth-century management theorist and practitioner, Mary Parker Follett. Though Greenleaf makes no mention of Follett that I have found, philosophically, the two were kindred spirits. Follett shared Greenleaf's idealism about the optimal working environment, but gave shape to her theory by proposing a series of principles that make the theoretical immediately applicable. Taken together, the Greenleaf-Follett tandem creates a philosophical and practical syncretism that underlies a leadership model particularly suited to the challenges higher education faces in the new century. It is a model that I predict eventually will dominate academic leadership, simply because those institutions that are not led by servants with savvy will have become, at best, ineffective, and at worst, obsolete.

Greenleaf titled his leadership philosophy *Servant Leadership,* and I will use that name throughout as I refer to his principles and writings. Follett was less inclined to labels—or practiced at a time when labeling was not as popular. One that has been applied to her principles by others has been "dynamic administration," and the description is apt. I have chosen to call the marriage of their ideas "syncretic leadership," the melding of two or more into one, with the combination yielding something uniquely stronger and more useful than the sum of the parts.

I have chosen not to provide a brief summary of each chapter in the preface. The topics are listed by chapter in the Table of Contents, and a quick thumb through of the book will give an immediate sense of what each discusses. The book has been organized, however, so that each chapter is progressive, but stands by itself as illustrating an important and discrete leadership lesson. It will be useful as both a personal guidebook to principles of leadership and as a text for those studying various approaches to leadership as an art and science.

For those who are just beginning their journeys as college leaders, let me repeat my mentor's observation that there is no perfect preparation for being ultimately responsible. College leadership is a very demanding job, and it is becoming more so each year. But the pressures and trials of those demands can be mitigated considerably if one enters the assignment fully committed to serving each person touched by the organization. To you old hands, for at least the next few hours, bridle your skepticism, contemplate the most critical challenges you face, and consider the possibility that each might best be addressed by calling the principal players together and asking, "How can we best resolve this in a way that helps each of us accomplish what we would like?" And while you are about it, take a moment to remember what you have dreamed—in those moments when you have allowed yourself to think about what you would like your institution to be if it could be anything you wished. That is where your vision needs to take you, but it will not happen unless you commit yourself to becoming a savvy servant—not just to your faculty, but to your students, to your community, and to society as a whole.

Institutional cultures are developed over decades, and changing them cannot be done in a matter of weeks. But all change begins with an initial commitment to new direction, and my intent in the pages that follow is to illustrate that the new direction in educational leadership will come through a complete commitment to service.

NOTE

1. James L. Fisher, *Power of the Presidency* (New York: Macmillan, 1984), 1.

ACKNOWLEDGMENTS

Much of the philosophy and conviction found in this book was inherited from my friend, colleague, and mentor, Jim Tatum. Jim first exposed me to the writings and thinking of Robert Greenleaf, to the ethical principles espoused by Rushworth Kidder, and to the personal introspection of Parker Palmer—all of whom Jim has known personally. Under his board leadership, we experimented with and applied various approaches to Servant Leadership as a college, and Jim and I spent hours discussing the application of various religious schools of thought to leading in higher education. He is specifically mentioned in the book in a number of places, but his voice is present throughout, and I am eternally grateful for his guidance and inspiration.

Special thanks are also due to my wife, Holly, who served as home editor and encourager, and to my assistant for many years, Gale Lynch, who read and critiqued early sections of the book. Deep appreciation also goes to my associates, Mary Beth Ottinger, Kimberly Allen, and Lois Stelpflug, for their research and editing assistance, and to Susan Slesinger for her invaluable editing and critique on behalf of the publisher. I am particularly grateful to the scholars and devotees who have preserved the work and legacies of Robert Greenleaf and Mary Parker Follett, whose insights form the foundation of this work, and to Mary Ann and Des Lee, whose generous support to the university and to my position made the writing of this book possible.

CHAPTER 1

The Need for New Leadership

Problems cannot be solved at the same level of awareness that created them.

—Albert Einstein

I t is time for a new approach to leadership in higher education in America. The world is changing rapidly around us, calling desperately for us to change with it and ease some of the burden of its own transformation. But we are either failing to hear the pleas, or are choosing to ignore them. Others are listening—others who have the wherewithal to respond, and are doing so. The window of opportunity for traditional higher education to meet the needs and challenges of a new century is narrowing, possibly to only a few short decades, and we must act before the opportunities to innovate have not all been usurped by other educational providers.

As the twenty-first century opened, the late Frank Newman and two colleagues with Brown University's Futures Project wrote a pointed critique of the failures of higher education to meet public needs for the *Review* supplement to the *Chronicle of Higher Education*, noting in its opening paragraph:

> Yet a dangerous gap is growing between what the public needs from higher education and how colleges and universities are serving those needs. The gap has received little attention within institutions because they lack clear measurements for their performance and because they are generally satisfied with the status quo. But if the gap is not closed, it will increasingly impede higher education's ability to serve the public and ultimately threaten colleges' ability to thrive and grow.[1]

The article goes on to outline seven areas where the writers maintain there is a "growing gap between the public's needs and the performance of colleges and universities...." The list includes the need to take responsibility for learning, to move beyond access to attainment, to be more effective and productive, to better support elementary and secondary education, to reduce conflict of interest in research, to serve as society's critic, and to rebuild political involvement to sustain democracy.[2]

Those who have been giving ear to critiques of higher education in recent years will find these familiar themes. A report published several years earlier by the National Center for Research in Vocational Education, headquartered at the University of California at Berkeley, began its Executive Summary by declaring:

> Change is not an option—it is an inevitability. And the tremendous changes in the culture that surrounds and impacts higher education have created both crisis and opportunity. As presently organized and delivered, higher education is no longer sustainable, technologically or pedagogically.[3]

These changes and their effects on higher education are by no means limited to vocational education. Shortly after this report was published, I attended a statewide conference on transfer and articulation that graphically illustrated the nature and immediacy of this crisis for all in the higher education community. The conference focused on a set of newly revised state guidelines describing how institutions should deal with students moving from one college to another within the same state, guidelines that had not been revised in over a decade. Several new developments showed the old rules to be inadequate, and pressure was building in the state legislature for immediate change. As the conference was in session, a resolution was making its way though the state's House of Representatives, mandating revisions within a month or the legislature would intervene.

One particularly animated and contentious debate occurred during an open meeting sponsored by the committee that had been charged by the State Coordinating Board with crafting the new guidelines. The session was an invitation to any member of the audience—higher education community or general public—to comment on the new recommendations. Most of the changes were minor, but when one particular issue was placed on the table, a line of concerned academics hurried to the podium. The item suggested revision of an old rule that limited the number of credits a student could transfer from a community college to a four-year institution to 64 hours. The committee was recommending that students be allowed to take as many "lower division" hours at community colleges as they wished, with all being eligible to transfer if they fit within the degree program.

Concerns from the floor revolved around two issues: what qualifies a course as "lower division," and what should be the expectation for students once they become enrolled in the "upper division" portion of their studies? A professor from one of the state's large urban universities argued eloquently that there was something so uniquely rich about the upper division experience at a four-year institution that to shorten it would be to shortchange a student's education.

"I can see the validity of accepting 90 hours in transfer from another *university*, but only 64 for a student coming from a community college, even if they both completed the same courses," he stated. "The community college student simply hasn't had the same exposure to the university's scholarly environment."

Another critic took a somewhat different tack. "We intentionally classify some courses as upper division because we want students to take them from us," she confided. "It is difficult to maintain program integrity if you can't require students to take a number of classes from your institution. Plus, many of us are developing missions with unique institutional flavors. We want students to spend enough time with us to appreciate that mission uniqueness."

As I listened to the debate from the back of the room, I was struck by how incongruous it was compared with the trends suggested by two articles sitting in the briefcase at my feet. Both were from recent issues of the *Chronicle of Higher Education*, and both suggested that our debate about traditional definitions and roles was missing the mark completely. One article, a cover story, reviewed the debate occurring in Arizona where the State Assembly was considering extending four-year degree programs in specific technical areas to community colleges. The public, or at least representatives of the public, were arguing that in some specialized programs, community colleges had greater experience and expertise than did their four-year counterparts. It made economic sense, they contended, to create baccalaureate degrees at these locations rather than start from scratch at one of the universities.

The two legislative sponsors of the Arizona bill explained that they were seeking low-cost, job-related degrees for workers whose lives were already so packed with commitments that two years at a distant university were simply out of the question.

"We want colleges to come and say, 'There are needs to be met, and we want to meet those needs,'" one sponsor stated. "If the universities aren't going to do it, step aside and let someone else do it."[4]

The second article, also a cover story, discussed the challenges facing what was then being developed as the Western Governors' University (WGU), and the implications its programs would have for the rest of higher education. This article seemed particularly out of sync with the debate going on in the room. If the Western Governors' experiment or something akin to it succeeded, students would be receiving degrees based not upon credit hours—upper or lower division—but upon a set of competencies. Students could demonstrate that they had mastered these competencies without ever setting foot in a classroom, entirely missing the experience of the academic environment so eloquently supported by the concerned professor.

Utah's governor at the time, Michael Leavitt, in a related article on the WGU experiment, described traditional higher education as "kind of a feudal system," clinging to its own currency, the credit hour, and being left behind by the newly emerging educational desires of the public. "This isn't something that we've invented," Leavitt said of the WGU creation. "The market is driving it. People are demanding it."[5]

The Western Governors' experiment had much greater difficulty getting off the ground than was anticipated, but has found new life in recent years. Other tradition-breaking models such as the University of Phoenix have been phenomenally successful. As I sat in the back of the committee room listening to the testimony and considering Leavitt's comments, I had the distinct feeling that, elsewhere, the world's academic reality was being reshaped at breakneck speed, while we at the conference were trying desperately to preserve a system that was not the least bit prepared to accommodate those changes.

Management theorist and organizational development specialist Peter Vaill argues that if the modern college or university is to survive in any form into the twenty-first century, several of these major shifts in philosophy and practice will be absolutely essential. He subtitles his book, *Learning as a Way of Being*, "Strategies for Surviving in a World of Permanent White Water," and compares today's chaotic leadership environment to rafting on a river of continuous rapids. Vaill is a systems theorist and maintains that systems such as higher education are more accurately described as "subsystems"—parts of dynamic macrosystems in which these complex systems run "because at millions of operational points, human will and human judgment are exercised, usually on behalf of the systems' objectives. The will and judgment are exercised *both by those operating the systems and by those who use them.*"[6] My observation, as I considered the dichotomy between the conference debate and the content of the articles in my briefcase, was that we in the academic subsystem are in the process of exercising will and judgments about our own future, with complete disregard for the will and judgment of those in the macrosystem who use our services.

Vaill illustrates the constant, essential interaction of subsystems within a macrosystem using the metaphor of a business trip and the many cooperative activities that lead to its success or failure. His illustration might just as easily have been an academic day for any of us in higher education, and I repeat Vaill's analogy here, making only the substitution for "a business trip" shown in parenthesis:

> Permanent white water metaphorically defines the difficult conditions under which people exercise their will and judgment within society's macrosystems. Virtually every person acting within the various systems that support (higher education) is coping with a continuing stream of changes that make operating his or her part of the system anything but routine. All of these people are under continuing pressure to improve performance and control costs. They are confronted constantly with new methods and technologies. Every one of them is working with new people in the system all the time, and the mix of people of different nationalities, ethnicities, religions, and gender is also increasing. All of them are experiencing great stress and complexity outside the job, living as they do in a society of burgeoning social problems such as drug abuse, crime, consumer debt, family conflicts, pollution, and racial and ethnic conflict. Despite the stress they are under, they are all being urged to innovate, to look for ways to improve the operation of the system, to upgrade their own skills, and to work more effectively with each other.... In effect,

even as they personally experience the ongoing impact of changes introduced by others, of permanent white water, they are creating permanent white water for others by the changes they themselves introduce. Turbulence and instability are woven into the macrosystem; they are not just things that happen to it from the outside.[7]

I once attended a workshop at which Vaill was a guest presenter, and during a small group "fireside chat," he invited each participant to create his or her own metaphor for a condition of continuous, unpredictable, and disruptive change. As a former military pilot, the one that immediately came to mind for me was <u>clear air turbulence.</u> I vividly remembered a knuckle-whitening five minutes during a training mission for student navigators I flew in the early 1970s. We were in an old T-29, the military version of the twin engine Convair 440 that for many years was the mainstay of small commuter airlines in the United States. The plane was as reliable as any in the Air Force inventory, but was a lumbering, noisy old bird we affectionately called The Astro-Pig.

On this particular flight, we had turned around over Kingman, Arizona and were flying back toward California's Mojave Desert. As we started across the Colorado River at 15,000 feet, an updraft suddenly threw the plane skyward, shooting us up at 1,500 feet per minute. Knowing that other planes were flying the same route but were coming toward us at higher altitudes, I pushed the throttles full against the stops and nosed over into what should have been a steep dive; but still the old plane soared upward. Then, almost 5,000 feet above our assigned altitude, we seemed to pause momentarily in the sky, then plunged downward with such a rapid descent that equipment flew to the ceiling and we were suspended in our shoulder straps. I yanked the nose from the dive position into what should have been a steep climb, still with power full-on, but the plane continued to drop as if free falling in a vacuum. After a 10,000-foot plunge, the propellers finally grabbed the air again and pulled us out of what all of us had decided was our final flying adventure.

Unlike white water, clear air turbulence cannot be seen or heard in the distance, but often takes the flyer completely by surprise, sometimes with fatal results. I would venture that every college or university president who has been in office for more than a year has experienced it; sudden institutional updrafts that unexpectedly throw the organization in one direction, followed by a heart-stopping pause—a "waiting for the other shoe to drop" moment—then a complete reversal, plunging the college downward in a dive that the leader fears he or she may not survive.

Whichever metaphor we choose to describe the unpredictable changes we are experiencing, higher education appears particularly ill-prepared to keep pace. Shortly after this adventure over the Colorado River, the Air Force transitioned from the old T-29 to Boeing 737s for navigator training, calling the new plane the T-43. The T-43 included new technology and new performance capabilities that could deal with the sudden wind shears we had experienced. Yet in higher education, we now find ourselves flying in constant clear air turbulence, but are electing to stay with the old faithful T-29, arguing that it has always stood us in good stead.

At the fireside chat with Peter Vaill mentioned earlier, Vaill responded to a question from a member of the group about the educational system's ability to adapt by commenting:

> There is this thing that you could call the "dinosaur" problem, where the world is evolving faster than the organism can keep up. So there comes a point where it is past the point where the organism can *ever* catch up. Now, any given dinosaur looks around and says, "I don't see what the problem is," but the third party up in the sky looks down and says, "Idiot! Your species is doomed!" I sometimes wonder about higher education—whether we are evolving—whether we are even close to evolving as fast as the environment is asking us to evolve, and whether there might come a time—sometime over the next probably no more than 20 years, and no longer than 50 years—when society just kind of looks around and says, "Oh, are you people still here?" Society has just kind of moved on, and we're like the fireman on the diesel locomotives.[8]

Vaill notes in his writing that "The problem with our existing model of learning is that it depicts learning as an institutional activity," defining institutional learning as that which is thoroughly institutionalized in its practice and philosophy, and still thinks of place in terms of bricks and mortar.[9] Neither of these attributes is consistent with the desires or goals of the University of Phoenix or WGU models, with the interests of much of the business and industrial community, or with the needs of a growing number of students. They are also out of tune with what we are seeing in our own distance learning enrollments, where we are all aware that online classes fill first, and students beg for more.

Businesses tell us that our old traditional product is not what they want—that students are not prepared for roles in the real world macrosystems in which business now operates without limitations of time or place. From students we hear that we are not offering what they need, when they need it, utilizing delivery methods with which they are increasingly adept. Our employees—those we serve internally—are insisting on greater voice, greater autonomy, and greater involvement in the decisions that affect their own personal goals.

Yet we have been among the most successful subsystems at doggedly resisting change. Why? The answers lie in part among some of higher education's most cherished traditions.

A number of the qualities and promises of academic life that we view as most sacred stand as major impediments to our abilities to adjust. Among these are intellectualism, misdirected collegiality, and our network of professional protections. Add to these higher education's traditional social isolationism, our tendency to be slow to adapt to new technologies, and a tendency to select leadership with these same, insulated views, and we have a formula for almost complete inertia.

For centuries many of these characteristics have stood the academy in good stead and it is difficult for us to now admit that they may have become obstacles.

Each of these characteristics merits mention, focusing most completely upon leadership since it is central to bringing about change in the other five attributes.

INTELLECTUALISM

Higher education *is* higher education because it has traditionally been the central repository for scholarship and knowledge. The academic community has collectively held what was considered to be the best secular understanding of the universe, the world and all that occurs within it, to the degree that it is accessible through human study. It has been the source, the wellspring of answers to social and scientific problems. To tell higher education that it is no longer effectively doing its job is like going to Delphi to inform the oracle that she doesn't know what she is talking about. We do not take criticism well, and even when we acknowledge the validity of a concern, we prefer to either pronounce a quick fix, based upon our understanding of the literature, or to massage it, debate it, turn it completely so that each facet can be evaluated before we even begin to *consider* change.

Thomas Kuhn in his 1970 masterpiece, *The Structure of Scientific Revolutions*, accurately observed that paradigm shifts do not occur until the evidence that they must do so overwhelms existing theory to the point that the old paradigm is crushed under the weight of the new. I recall in-depth discussions of Kuhn's observations in at least a half-dozen graduate courses, yet we have completely failed to see that they apply equally to our own inability to change paradigms. We are particularly adept at shaping discordant information to our existing models, supporting the old paradigms even though the sheer weight of change-demanding data threatens revolutionary rather than evolutionary change.[10]

COLLEGIALITY

One of the great strengths of the higher education community is that many within it are empowered to help shape the nature of their work. In particular, the faculty has considerable say about what a department or discipline views as important, and how it converts those beliefs into program offerings and behaviors. For those institutions in which they play an appropriate role, research and scholarly writing, as long as they are viewed as "productive" in some generic sense, are left largely to the discretion of departments and individual faculty. I would not choose to change this collegiality and independence, and it is one of the major reasons I elected to make my professional home in higher education. But with ability to change now critical to our professional survival, collegiality sometimes gets in the way.

In an article in *Business Horizons*, the journal of the School of Business at Indiana University, Joseph and Bettie Stanislao outline a series of personnel-based obstacles to change, dividing them between "persons having veto power" and "persons having no veto power." Obviously, those with veto power are in the best position to resist change, and the collegial nature of higher education places an unusually high percentage of its professional ranks in this category.

Those holding veto power may resist change, the Stanislaos observe, for any of a half-dozen reasons. They may desire inertia (wish to keep things as they are because of the comfort level), fear the unknown, feel insecure or fear failure or obsolescence, resent changes in an area in which they have a personal stake, or have personality conflicts with the person wishing to initiate change. I am reminded of a saying I hear often in the halls of the state legislature that, "It is much easier to kill a bill than it is to pass one." The same can be said for any new approach in the academy. When many have veto power, and when each may have any number of reasons to keep things as they are, it is much easier to prevent change than to enact it. Higher education, by the nature of its organization, places many in positions to impede change, and experience shows that some are always willing to exercise this prerogative.

PROFESSIONAL PROTECTIONS

No profession has developed a more complete and effective network of professional protections than has higher education. We have tenure, professional rank, campus-based faculty associations and unions, national advocacy groups at both the disciplinary and professional level, and the standard series of due process procedures. Some states have placed mandatory "shared governance" into statute, giving a variety of groups check-and-balance authority on policy matters. Each of these protections was created to serve a useful purpose, but in combination, they have given some feelings of invulnerability in the face of the need to change and have made significant change difficult to enact. Groups and individuals can refuse with impunity, even when changes are clearly viewed by the majority of others as being in the best interest of the institution. The leader who declares, "We are going to do it this way, or else…" often finds that the "or else" means, "We are going to stay the same way, but with new leadership."

SOCIAL AND CULTURAL ISOLATION

It is quite possible for a college professor or administrator to spend an entire professional life without ever working outside of the academy. Professors of elementary education can become nationally recognized specialists without spending a day in a classroom as a full-time teacher, marketing professors without developing a "real life" promotional campaign, and PhDs in business without ever working in a for-profit organization. Many are pure theoreticians, long on principle but short on practice. As a result, we are inclined to see issues and deal with them as abstractions rather than as practical problems that demand concrete and immediate solutions.

In certain cases, this lack of exposure to "the real world" limits the options we are able to see, but a college development officer who came to development work from the business world once commented to me that he saw just the opposite problem in education. He believed that instead of social isolation limiting the possibilities professors would consider, it encouraged them to see and consider all possibilities equally. It frustrated him, he said, to have lunch with his academic colleagues, because they seemed to have such a limited sense of what was practical and what was not. "If you raise an issue with this bunch—whether a problem or an opportunity—they always attack it in the same way," he said. "They begin by taking it apart, poking holes in it to see where the soft spots are. Then they turn it this way and that, thinking of every conceivable way of looking at the issue. If it's an opportunity, they come up with a hundred reasons it won't work. If it's a problem, they'll tell you a dozen reasons that it really isn't a problem. It helps to see all sides of the issue, but they never get a damn thing decided. And they don't seem to have the faintest understanding that people are having to find real solutions to these issues every day and act on them."

Hunter Rawlings, while serving as president of the University of Iowa, chided his colleagues at an annual Liberal Arts Faculty Assembly as being too secure in their place of privilege, insulated from the grinding poverty and hopelessness of America's cities, and insensitive to the problems of over-crowded public schools and teachers who had to struggle daily with crushing teaching loads and unruly discipline.[11] He suggested that the university would not be able to effectively address pertinent public issues until there was a greater sense in higher education of what these issues are all about in the real world.

This insulation, this ability to separate ourselves from real issues and challenges by turning them into theoretical abstractions, is a powerful academic tool and a critical part of the training many of us received that emphasized dispassionate examination and critical analysis. It also becomes a significant handicap when an issue affecting our own survival demands immediate action and response. We currently stand at one of those critical junctures, and are being paralyzed by our inability to separate the real from abstract theoretical constructs.

TECHNICAL NAÏVETÉ

At a conference at which Willard Daggett, president of the International Center for Leadership in Education, was the keynote speaker, Daggett asserted that academics are among the slowest in our society to accept and gain skill with new technologies. As a result, those who have demands for our services are often far more technologically astute than we are, and come to us expecting the same level of technological savvy. They find that we are often a generation behind in our equipment and several technological generations behind in our know-how.[12]

This aversion to technological change will not suit us well if Peter Drucker accurately saw our future. In the early days of distance education, he noted, "Already we are beginning to deliver more lectures and classes off campus via satellite or two-way video at a fraction of the cost. The college won't survive as a residential institution. Today's buildings are hopelessly unsuited and totally unneeded."[13]

A long-time colleague resolutely refuses to read e-mail, insisting that it dehumanizes communication. He is constantly irritated about being "left out of the loop," and believes that he is intentionally being marginalized when, in fact, he is simply not keeping abreast of what has become the primary information dissemination network in the world. Technology is revolutionizing higher education for those who will utilize it, and those who use our services are expecting its utilization. As a "final thought" in a white paper on the topic of education and technology, Daggett wrote, "We need to look closely today at how and what we teach, and we must be prepared to recognize how that mix needs to change. The question is: How will schools accomplish this? There is no easy fix or pat answer to this question, but we must pursue it—honestly and courageously—in order to prepare our students for the world of tomorrow."[14]

TRADITIONAL APPROACHES TO LEADERSHIP

Traditionally, leadership in the academy has not only come from within, but from the ranks of those who have been most susceptible to the barriers to change listed above: the faculty. We have long held that scholars should lead colleges, a belief that I support in large part. There are numerous examples of nonacademics being selected to lead higher education institutions, and they are as likely to ignore and downplay the importance of maintaining academic integrity as the academics are to downplay the necessity to change, adapt, and be publicly responsive. Academic leadership must be thoroughly grounded in teaching and learning, and we must err on this side when making presidential selections. We must realize, however, that in accepting this line of succession, we accept that our leaders will have been nurtured in the very philosophies that make us change resistant.

Arthur Bentley noted in his turn of the century work on leadership, *The Process of Government*, that "leadership is not an affair of the individual leader. It is fundamentally an affair of the group."[15] Bentley saw leadership as essentially an *expression* of the group, and there are few places where this is more the case than in higher education. We have been inclined to expect our leadership to preserve and sustain rather than to modify, and deans and presidents who view themselves as change agents often find that they are at odds with the core of the establishment.

Yet we face a time of change by necessity. If we are to find leaders who can direct us through the maze of challenges that surely faces major efforts to transform higher education, we must either rethink our concept of leadership and transform existing leaders, or find leaders who bring fresh approaches and new vision. In Chapter 5, we will discuss Jim Collins's assertion that the very best leadership often does exist within the organization, but will also point out that these potential "level 5" leaders are just as often overlooked, intentionally ignored, or marginalized because of their progressive vision. Drucker describes the needed leader of today as one who has intellectual integrity, by which he means one with "the ability to see the world as it is, not as you want it to be." He adds, "They are servants of the organization—whether elected or appointed, whether the organization is a government, a government agency, a business, a hospital, a diocese. It is their duty to subordinate their likes, wishes, preferences to the welfare of the institution."[16] Too often in our profession, the emerging leader who tries to present the world to us as it is, is not the one we want to listen to, and selection committees lean toward the safer choice—the presidential candidate who will not rock the boat.

I need to make it clear here that I believe many of the values of our profession *are* timeless, that there is an academic integrity that must be preserved. A sense of what constitutes "an educated person" can be too easily trivialized or sacrificed to pragmatism. For these reasons, we need to seek to transform our existing leadership and to find new change-oriented leaders within, then empower them to transform us. We must embrace an approach to leadership that honors collegiality, but is sufficiently skilled to bring consensus to critical change strategies—leadership that widens our sense of inclusiveness and draws in those from other subsystems with which we must interact. We must reevaluate the professional protections we enjoy to determine if they continue to serve us well in a new climate of required flexibility and adaptability.

A university-based colleague with whom I reviewed the concerns outlined above was incensed that I suggested higher education has approached a state of crisis and is resistant to change.

"If one reads the history of higher education," he noted, "it would be difficult to find a moment when someone did not think we were in a crisis." As for our ability to change, he referenced a statement by Peter Drucker whom I had been citing as part of my own position, noting that in his 1985 book, *Innovation and Entrepreneurship,* Drucker stated that no better text for a history of entrepreneurship could be found than the creation of the modern American university.

He is right, of course, about the constant cry of wolf within the academy. We are always in a state of crisis in someone's mind, making it all the more difficult to assess when the condition actually exists, and even more difficult to convince others of that condition, once present. But assuming that Drucker was being appropriately quoted in this 1985 reference, one of the telling signs of impending crisis must be that by the time of his death, this important management theorist and visionary saw the modern university as highly vulnerable to our current whirlwind of change. In the 1997 article in *Forbes* cited above, Drucker is quoted as saying, "Thirty years from now the big university campuses will be relics. Universities won't survive. It's as large a change as when we first got the printed book." After noting that the cost of higher education is rising as rapidly as is health care, Drucker adds, "Such totally uncontrollable expenditures, without any visible improvement in either the content or the quality of education, means that the system is rapidly becoming untenable. Higher Education is in deep crisis."[17]

This book is about identifying or creating the transformational leadership needed to guide our colleges and universities through that permanent white water. It is about finding or building leaders who can look beyond the narrow subculture of the internal workings of the organization, to embrace the needs of an ever-expanding circle of cooperating systems that make up our social and professional universe. It postulates that leadership based on power, hierarchy, and control wears blinders due to the very nature of the leadership approach—blinders that eliminate options, limit alternatives, and thwart change. The new leadership must be a leadership based upon service—service to the college, service to faculty, service to students, and to the greater community.

A commitment to service removes the blinders of self, of control, and of predisposition to method. It assumes that all paths may be explored if they have the potential to lead us to a place where all served will be, to paraphrase Robert Greenleaf, wiser, healthier, more autonomous, and better able themselves to serve.[18] But it must be a service accompanied by a management savvy that astutely marshals resources, creates efficiencies, and rewards personal investment by others, while refusing to tolerate intransigence. The quote that opened this chapter suggests that problems cannot be solved with the same level of awareness that created them. This commitment to service first, with management savvy provides the new awareness needed to attack problems our old thinking created, but has been unable to solve. It frees us to allow our new awareness to evolve as additional challenges emerge.

NOTES

1. Frank Newman, Lara Couturier, and Jamie Scurry, "Higher Education Isn't Meeting the Public's Needs," *Chronicle of Higher Education*, 15 October 2004, B6.

2. Ibid.

3. George H. Copa and William Ammentorp, "A New Vision for the Two-Year Institution of Higher Education," *New Designs for the Two-Year Institution of Higher Education*, Executive Summary Report from the National Council for Research in Vocational Education, Fall 1997, http://newdesigns.oregonstate.edu/updates/MDS-1109/section02.html (accessed March 20, 2005).

4. Patrick Healy, "Arizona Considers Landmark Plan to Allow Community Colleges to Offer Baccalaureate Degrees," *Chronicle of Higher Education*, 16 January 1998, A30.

5. Goldie Blumenstyk, "Utah's Governor Enjoys Role as a Leading Proponent of Distance Learning," *Chronicle of Higher Education*, 6 February 1998, A23.

6. Peter Vaill, *Learning as a Way of Being* (San Francisco: Jossey-Bass, 1996), 6.

7. Ibid., 6–7.

8. Peter Vaill, "A Fireside Chat with Peter Vaill," *Peter Vaill Presentation*, (Robert K. Greenleaf Center for Servant-Leadership, 1996), audio cassette recording.

9. Vaill, *Learning as a Way of Being*, 32.

10. Thomas Kuhn, *The Structure of Scientific Revolutions* (Chicago: University of Chicago Press, 1970).

11. Charles Bullard, "Rawlings: Reject Greed and begin Era of Giving," *Des Moines Register*, 22 August 1990, A10.

12. Willard R. Daggett, "Academic and Technical Skills for the 21st Century" (speech, 11th Annual Building Bridges Conference, Missouri Department of Elementary and Secondary Education, Lake of the Ozarks, MO, 16 November 2004).

13. Robert Lenzner and S. Johnson, "Seeing Things as They Really Are," *Forbes*, 10 March 1997, 122–128, http://proquest.umi.com/pqdweb?index=48&did=11131941&SrchMode=3&sid=2&Fmt=3&VInst=PROD&VType=PQD&RQT=309&VName=PQD&TS=1150812178&clientId=45249&aid=1 (accessed November 7, 2005).

14. Willard R. Daggett, *Technology 2008: Preparing our Students for Our Changing World*, http://www.leadered.com/pdf/Technology%20White%20Paper.pdf.

15. Arthur F. Bentley, *The Process of Government* (Chicago: University of Chicago Press, 1908), 225.

16. Lenzner and Johnson.

17. Lenzner and Johnson.

18. Robert K. Greenleaf, *The Servant as Leader* (Indianapolis: Robert K. Greenleaf Center, 1991), 7.

CHAPTER

Leadership as a Quest to Serve

I don't know what your destiny will be but one thing I know: the only ones among you who will be really happy are those who have sought and found how to serve.

—Albert Schweitzer

During a workshop for educational leaders some years ago at which I had been asked to discuss Greenleaf's principles of Servant-Leadership, I attempted to find an illustration that would show how fully the college at which I worked viewed the principle of leadership as service. I explained that each year, everyone within the organization was invited to evaluate the chief executive officer (CEO). All employees had an opportunity to respond to a number of open-ended questions about areas of needed improvement, and these evaluations—warts and all—were sent in summary form directly to the governing board.

Following the session, a fellow college president cornered me and said with a trace of testiness, "When I start working for the janitors, they can evaluate me." Obviously, my colleague had missed the entire point of my presentation. As a CEO or senior administrator, a college leader *does* work for the custodians—and the secretaries, the food services personnel, the graduate assistants, and the work-study students who monitor the open computer labs. Leadership is an act of service, and the more responsible the leadership position, the more complete the obligation to serve. The principle applies to business, to education, and to government, despite a growing cynicism in our country that is leading people to believe that business focuses on making money at everyone's expense and that "government service" is an oxymoron. Much of the cynicism is, in fact, a reflection of the public's perception that service is no longer central to leadership.

My focus in this book is solely on educational leadership. I know it best, and it seems to most naturally lend itself to servant-centered leadership approaches. Our product as educators is human growth and improvement of the human condition—economically, intellectually and socially. Most of our mission statements contain references to "serving, aiding, assisting, and developing." Yet, so much administrative time is spent wooing donors, protecting turf, courting legislators and complying with regulation that much of the visionary passion has been drained from the position and profession. It is time to find it again, and a scattered few—just enough to begin to attract attention—are rediscovering the spark needed to reignite a passion for leadership based on service. They are discovering that truly satisfying, problem-solving, and continuously productive leadership is a stewardship, a calling. Not a divine calling perhaps, but a spiritual one, nonetheless. It strikes a chord at the very core of their being and forces them to ask questions about the value and the values of work, about what is fair and honest and right, as well as what is "productive."

Use of the word "spiritual" immediately makes many uneasy, fearing that I am somehow trying to draw doctrinaire religious discussion into this review of leadership. On the contrary, I am thinking of spiritual as another term for metaphysical—for that experience that falls outside of the physical, measurable world and touches at that part of us that cannot easily be defined by, or limited to, physical description.

Writing in the *Washington Post,* Don Oldenburg described his discovery of several of these leaders, though his examples were principally from business. He reminded us in the opening paragraphs of his piece of the early scenes of the film *Jerry Maguire,* in which Maguire, a hard driving, bottom-line sports agent, experienced a soul-wrenching epiphany and spent the rest of that night writing a personal "mission statement." In this statement, Maguire renounced greed, espoused taking more time and making less money, caring about clients, and returning the passion to the job. His colleagues, feeling the same pricks of conscience and lack of fulfillment, applauded his efforts, but abandoned him when management fired the idealistic Maguire.

Oldenburg went on to explain that a number of real life Maguires have surfaced in the business world—people desperate to return meaning to what they are doing and joy to how they do it. He introduced us to ad executives, business consultants, and corporate leaders who had begun to speak of "spirit in work" and "heart connection" in working relationships. People, he said, are yearning for meaning and fulfillment in their jobs, moving by inference the role of leadership more directly to that of creating a working environment in which meaning and fulfillment can be rediscovered.[1]

Essayist and children's author E. B. White seemed to be explaining this basic human desire to find fulfillment in all aspects of life in a letter to a young reader named Jill, who had written White following the publication of his children's story *Stuart Little*. The tale is about a mouse who undertakes a quest in search of the bird Margelo, Stuart Little's vision of all that is good and beautiful in the world. Its publication created quite a stir among parents, teachers, and children because at the story's end, Stuart has been unable to find Margelo and still hasn't made his way home. Jill wrote to White to express her concern for Stuart's welfare, and received a reply in which White explained:

> "Stuart Little" is the story of a quest or search. Much of life is questing and searching, and I was writing about that. If the book ends while the search is still going on, that's because I wanted it that way. As you grow older you will realize that many of us in this world go through life looking for something that seems beautiful and good—often something we can't quite name. In Stuart's case, he was searching for the bird Margelo, who was his idea of beauty and goodness. Whether he ever found her or not, or whether he ever got home or not, is less important than the adventure itself.[2]

Stephen Covey acknowledges this sense of "calling" when he describes principle-centered leaders as those who "see life as a mission, not as a career. Their nurturing sources have armed and prepared them for service."[3] Covey's book, *Principle-Centered Leadership*, and much of his subsequent writing, is dedicated to identifying the characteristics of these leaders and the motives and experiences that incline them toward service as the center of, and as a centering activity for their leadership approach.

The sense that work, including leadership roles, should incorporate this quest for goodness and beauty is certainly not original with me, with Covey, or with those recognized in Oldenburg's *Washington Post* article. It predates Jesus' council that he who wishes to be greatest among us should be servant to others, and appears in the early Buddhist teaching of right action, the Confucian concepts of *li* and *jen,* and in the wisdom of the Taoist sage Lao Tzu. For some, this might suggest that the quest for service in leadership is largely religious. Yet, at least the oriental philosophies mentioned are as easily social and political as religious, and social and political leaders such as Gandhi and Martin Luther King demonstrated how readily an element of spirituality can be transferred to secular leadership.

ROBERT GREENLEAF AND SERVANT-LEADERSHIP

In recent years, the concept of the leader as servant has been given clearest voice by Robert K. Greenleaf, an AT&T executive during the decades of the 1950s through 70s. Greenleaf recognized in his own work, and in corporate America in general, the need for a new leadership based upon total concern for all served by the organization. While working as director of Management Research for AT&T, Greenleaf held joint appointments at Massachusetts Institute of Technology's Sloan School of Management and at Harvard Business School as visiting lecturer, and served as consultant to major universities and corporations on leadership and management. He is generally credited with having coined the name "Servant-Leadership" with his seminal essay, *The Servant as Leader.*

Greenleaf attributed the initial inspiration for his servant-leader philosophy to a reading of Hermann Hesse's *Journey to the East,* a fictional account of a group of travelers on a spiritual quest. While journeying, the group is assisted by a servant, Leo, who is the central figure of Hesse's tale. During the course of the journey, Leo suddenly leaves the group, and it finds that it immediately begins to disintegrate. The travelers eventually abandon their journey, realizing that the servant Leo's selfless service had been the glue that held the group together, giving it unity and focus. One of the travelers, wandering on his own, eventually reaches the home of the order that initially sponsored the group's journey and finds, to his dismay, that Leo is the order's head and spiritual guide. In *The Servant as Leader* Greenleaf observes:

> To me, this story clearly says that *the great leader is seen as servant first,* and that simple fact is key to his greatness. Leo was actually the leader all the time, but he was servant first because that was what he was, *deep down inside.* Leadership was bestowed upon a man who was by nature a servant. It was something given, or assumed, that could be taken away. His servant nature was the real man, not bestowed, not assumed, and not to be taken away. He was servant first. (Italics are Greenleaf's.)[4]

Greenleaf read the account of Leo 11 years before beginning to formulate his thoughts on Servant-Leadership. During the interim, he found, as he worked in consulting capacities with corporations and universities, that the nation was, in his judgment, in the midst of a leadership crisis. In his opening essay, he explained that he felt his own personal quest must be a commitment to do what he could about this crisis. His mission, he believed, was to help the serving person overcome the tendency to "deny wholeness and creative fulfillment for themselves by failing to lead when they could lead."[5]

What is the servant-leader in Greenleaf's mind? The "servant-first" leader is a person of faith—faith as defined by Dean Inge as "the choice of the nobler hypothesis."[6] And the nobler hypothesis is that the true leader strives first to listen and understand, to accept and to empathize, to seek to build community based upon trust and respect, mutual growth and fulfillment. The greater hypothesis suggests that the leader must always be engaged in living out a great dream for the organization, for its members, and for those it serves based upon a collective vision of what the organization *should* be. The leader continually asks, "Does this institution create an environment through which each person touched by its activity—client, employee, community supporter—comes away from that experience with greater personal freedom, with a greater sense of accomplishment of his or her own personal vision, and with greater commitment to service?" To use Greenleaf's words, "Do those served grow as persons; do they, while being served, become healthier, wiser, freer, more autonomous, more likely themselves to become servants?"[7]

In addition to the organizational skills, visionary insights, and charismatic personality we typically associate with leadership, Greenleaf places great value on an intuitive sense, what he calls "a sense for the unknowable," and on an ability to "foresee the unforeseeable."[8] He expresses this in later writing as recognition of the need for "spirit" in work—a spirituality based on this nobler hypothesis and the leader's desire to help the organization know and do what is right.

> The primary responsibility of an organization, according to Greenleaf, is peo-ple-building. Some institutions achieve distinction for a short time by the intelligent *use* of people; but it is not a happy achievement, and eminence, so derived, does not last long. Others aspire to distinction (or the reduction of problems) by embracing "gimmicks": profit sharing, work enlargement, information, participation, suggestion plans, paternalism, motivational man-agement. Nothing wrong with these in a people-building institution. But in a people-using institution they are like aspirin—sometimes stimulating and pain relieving, and they may produce an immediate measurable improvement of sorts. But these are not the means whereby an institution moves from people-using to people-building. In fact, an overdose of these nostrums may seal an institution's fate as a people-user for a very long time.
>
> An institution starts on a course toward people-building with leadership that has a firmly established context of *people first*. With that, the right action falls naturally into place. And none of the conventional gimmicks may ever be used.[9]

In later essays such as "The Institution as Servant," "The Teacher as Servant," and "Trustees as Servants," Greenleaf applies these principles specifically to educational leadership, though most of his own leadership and management experience was in the business sector. He was particularly sensitive to the role of the university because of its responsibilities to teach, train, and nurture future leaders—an area where he believed the academic community had largely failed. Their focus, he argued in a series of lectures delivered to the Dartmouth Alumni College in 1969, had been too much on practice and too little on principle. Greenleaf's concerns were undoubtedly shaped by the times, the late 1960s, when antiestablishment attitudes among students and faculty alike discouraged much discussion at all of principle in the academy. He argued, nonetheless, that lead-ership needed to be based upon four essentials: values, goals, competence and spirit, and that the leader must be primus inter pares—first among equals.[10] These essentials underlie much of the rest of Greenleaf's significant body of writing on Servant-Leadership.

Larry Spears, Executive Director of the Greenleaf Center, and editor of much of Greenleaf's work, has identified within these writings 10 critical characteristics of the servant-leader: Listening, empathy, healing, awareness, persuasion, con-ceptualization, foresight, stewardship, commitment to the growth of people, and community building.[11] Of these 10, the first 7 are what I would consider *abilities*, while the last 3 are *responsibilities*, the ability to respond appropriately on behalf of the organization being served.

Many have argued that there is an idealism in this list and in Servant-Leadership that renders it impractical. To some degree, I too find Greenleaf's formula for

applying it to the academic community to be unrealistic, and in some ways symp-
tomatic of why colleges change so slowly. His ultimate view of primus inter pares
is one of institutional governance through a council of peers. "There is," he stated,
"still a 'first,' a leader, but he is not the chief. The difference may appear to be
subtle, but it is important that the *primus* constantly tests and proves his leadership
among a group of able peers." Greenleaf admonished in his essay, "The Institution
as Servant," that universities change from the traditional hierarchical model with
one CEO to a team of equals with a primus. This team should consist of both
conceptualizers and operationalizers, those who can see and articulate the vision,
and those who can carry it out. The primus, Greenleaf believed, should be the
most skilled team builder among the group.[12]

This concept, though admirable in a pure, integrating way, ignores several
practicalities of academic life and leadership. The first is that, whether we would
like it to be the case or not, there is a necessity for someone to be ultimately
responsible—particularly when things are not going well. Even though a group
may be reaching decisions collectively and exercising some method of consensus
building, if consensus is not reached or if the decisions of the team do not prove
to be successful, we do not blame the team. We recognize that the primus is not
effectively coordinating action, drawing out ideas, and moving the group toward
an appropriate synthesis of those ideas and actions. In those cases we say that we
"do not have good leadership." Once that admission is made, we have essentially
acknowledged that we did not, in actuality, have inter pares (among equals), but
have placed greater weight of responsibility upon one individual. *When leadership change is necessary, we do not get rid of everyone and start over, but seek new
leadership*—immediately assigning to that newly selected person a larger share of
responsibility for success than we place on others. The inter pares must, by practicality, be attitudinal rather than organizational, and must be a characteristic of
the leader rather than of the organizational structure.

Greenleaf did acknowledge that institutional change and development generally rely upon the single leader, often working in the early stages of organizational
transformation as an evangelist, as something of "the voice of one crying in the
wilderness." In these early stages, few may understand the vision, and even fewer
may want to participate fully in bringing it about. In this more pragmatic manifestation of Servant-Leadership, Greenleaf acknowledged that the primus must carry
much of the responsibility, but consciously strive to create an air of inter pares
within the leadership team by soliciting complete input and acknowledging its
worth as being equal to his or her own. Over time, a more complete inter pares can
be achieved, but in a practical sense, the selected leader must always be primus.

A CALL FOR NEW LEADERSHIP

There are those who maintain that even with this practical concession to the
need for a single leader, Servant-Leadership remains impractical and counterpro-
ductive given the realities of today's highly politicized academy with adversarial

unionism, the litigious environment in which we work, and the cutthroat struggle for resources. I believe that, to a large degree, these challenges are but reflections of the crisis in leadership Greenleaf lamented, a crisis that will not be addressed and resolved without risk, courage, and approaches to leading which radically alter the ways we think, relate, and do.

The highly politicized academy, adversarial working relationships, and a litigious approach to problem solving have developed because we have *lacked* service- and spirit-centered leadership. I must admit, though, that Greenleaf's Servant-Leadership lacks practical dimension, and I plan to add that ingredient as I integrate it with Follett's pragmatic principles.

But to return to service-centered leadership, even in this syncretic form, it will take courage and a willingness to risk, to share power while remaining responsible, to become prey to those who want to resist, and to recognize that leadership based upon service makes the leader particularly vulnerable. The syncretic leader must be willing to assume responsibility for collaboratively made decisions. He or she must open the environment to invite and accept the best thoughts of everyone served, yet when the recommendation does not seem right, must firmly pursue what is. When things do not work as planned, the leader must be willing to step forward and say, "This happened on my watch and the responsibility is mine."

Walt Whitman begins his poem, "Song of the Open Road," with: "Afoot and light hearted I take to the open road, healthy, free, the world before me—the long brown path before me, leading me wherever I choose." It closes somewhat more cautiously with Whitman noting in one of the closing stanzas: "Now understand me well—It is provided in the essence of things that from any fruition of success, no matter what, shall come forth something to make a greater struggle necessary."[13]

I personally find great comfort in my conviction that this greater struggle *can* lead higher education in the direction most of us would choose to go anyway, given absolute choice—toward greater meaning in what we do, greater fulfillment in doing it, and greater satisfaction in the result. And we do have that choice. We can recapture the vision and zeal that fired our own early excitement about becoming servants in the field of education. We can extend that servant-first enthusiasm into building new leadership approaches that will transform our institutions, our profession, and public confidence in what we do.

Albert Camus entitled his last published lecture "Create Dangerously," and closed it with these thoughts, quoted by Greenleaf in his *Servant as Leader* essay:

> One may long, as I do, for a gentler flame, a respite, a pause for musing. But perhaps there is no other peace for the artist than what he finds in the heat of combat. 'Every wall is a door,' Emerson correctly said. Let us not look for the door, and the way out, anywhere but in the wall against which we are living. Instead, let us seek the respite where it is—in the thick of battle. For in my opinion, and this is where I shall close, it is there. Great ideas, it has been said, come into the world as gently as doves. Perhaps, then, if we listen attentively, we shall hear, amid the uproar of empires and nations, a faint

flutter of wings, the gentle stirring of life and hope. Some will say this hope lies in a nation, others, in a man. I believe rather that it is awakened, revived, nourished by millions of solitary individuals whose deeds and works every day negate frontiers and the crudest implications of history. As a result, there shines forth fleetingly the ever-threatened truth that each and every man, on the foundations of his own sufferings and joys, builds for them all.[14]

Leadership, like philosophy and literature, must be an art, the leader being one of the artists of whom Camus spoke. Perhaps there is no other respite for the leader than to find it in the heat of battle. If so, this is a call to arms. It is an invitation to the thousands who serve as educational leaders to find, in that wall of internal groundlessness and dissatisfaction, of public concern and cynicism, a door of redirected vision based on service to *each* individual—with the leader as principal servant.

It would be both presumptuous and dishonest to suggest that I have the perfect formula for doing so. Rather, I am hoping in the remaining pages to lead a conversation, share ideas, and point to successes. As an art, leadership, like vision, is a highly personal endeavor, and each approach to this syncretic leadership will be individually fashioned. It is not an approach that lends itself to formulaic books or lists of techniques. It is primarily an attitude of shared respect and mutual interest put into action through the use of a few, highly intuitive principles.

A college trustee who attended a workshop on Servant-Leadership offered by Robert Greenleaf's foundation commented upon his return that Servant-Leadership *could not* be reduced to formula. It was far too intrinsic, too personal. Dr. Pamela Walker, a California based academic administrator and researcher on Servant-Leadership, has wondered if it can, in fact, be taught at all. Is the quest to serve, she wonders, something that must first be so deeply felt by the individual that it compels the leader to seek to serve? Or is a desire to change institutional climate and activity sufficient motivation to lead one to become servant-first?[15]

My initial exposure to Greenleaf and my first experiences with Servant-Leadership inclined me to believe that Walker's first supposition might be the more accurate, that the quest to serve must first be so deeply felt that one is drawn to this approach to leadership. Greenleaf's description of the servant-led organization seemed so idealistically collaborative, so perfectly participatory, that I seriously wondered if it could be achieved without starting from scratch with a carefully screened group, selected primarily on the basis of wanting to work with this model. I have since learned that there are practical changes that can be made in any organization to accommodate and encourage service-centered leadership. Management principles such as those espoused by the forerunner of the modern management revolution, Mary Parker Follett, discussed in Chapter 4, give surprising practicality to leadership as service and create a more energized and practical syncretic whole.

I am also willing to believe that the vast majority of those of us who have chosen this profession did so out of a desire to serve, and have abiding hope—the hope expressed by Václav Havel when he said, "Hope forces me to believe that those better alternatives will prevail, and above all it forces me to do something to make them happen."[16] I do not see traditional leadership models enduring, partly because they are no longer perceived as producing that success and good-ness desired by the public, and partly because they are not suited to a new century where there will be growing expectations of equality, inclusiveness, participation, and change.

Consider what our measures of "good" and "effective" leadership have been in the past, and what leadership approaches have met the standards of those measures. In assessing past effectiveness, would we not include among the most significant questions: "How enduring have the effects of the leadership been?" and "How positive have those effects been on the development of civilization?" If so, service-centered leadership *has* been the most enduring and influential leader-ship approach in recorded history. It is simply time to rediscover it and apply its principles to education.

NOTES

1. Don Oldenburg, "Spirituality at Work," *Washington Post*, 15 April 1997, D5.

2. E. B. White, *Letters of E. B. White*, ed. Dorothy Lobrano Guth (New York: Harper & Row, 1989), 651–652.

3. Stephen R. Covey, *Principle-Centered Leadership* (New York: Simon & Schuster, 1990), 34.

4. Robert K. Greenleaf, *The Servant as Leader* (Indianapolis, IN: Robert K. Greenleaf Center, 1991), 2.

5. Robert K. Greenleaf, *The Servant-Leader Within: A Transformative Path*, ed. Larry C. Spears et al. (New York: Paulist Press, 2003), 31.

6. Dean Inge, *The Things That Remain* (New York: HarperCollins, 1958), 104.

7. Greenleaf, *The Servant as Leader*, 7.

8. Greenleaf, *The Servant as Leader*, 14.

9. Greenleaf, *The Servant as Leader*, 30–31.

10. Robert K. Greenleaf, *On Becoming a Servant Leader*, eds. Don M. Frick and Larry C. Spears (San Francisco: Jossey-Bass, 1996), 287–338.

11. Larry C. Spears, *Reflections of Leadership*, ed. Larry C. Spears (New York: John Wiley & Sons, 1995), 5–7.

12. Robert Greenleaf, *The Institution as Servant*, (Indianapolis: Robert K. Greenleaf Center, 1972), 11–17.

13. Walt Whitman, *Walt Whitman: Complete Poetry and Selected Prose and Letters*, ed. Emory Holloway (London: Nonesuch Press, 1967), 136–146.

14. Albert Camus, *Resistance, Rebellion and Death*, trans. Justin O'Brien (New York: Alfred A. Knopf, 1961), 272.

15. Pamela Walker, "A Case Study on Servant Leadership" (EdD diss., University of San Francisco, School of Education, 1997).

16. Lance Morrow, "I Cherish a Certain Hope," *Time*, 3 August 1992, 46.

CHAPTER

Lessons from the Wisdom Traditions

The highest truth cannot be put into words. Therefore the greatest teacher has nothing to say. He simply gives himself in service, and never worries.

—Tao Te Ching

In closing the last chapter, I was bold enough to suggest that much of the leadership practice common in today's organizations cannot endure. The world has become too small, too much Marshall McLuhan's "global village."[1] It is a world in which affluence and poverty, authoritarianism and egalitarianism, isolationist views and the need to collaborate can no longer coexist without a rumbling, festering expectation that there should be greater opportunity to participate. Communism appears to have failed as a solution, but top-down capitalism is also struggling, giving way to systems that have managed to incorporate greater inclusiveness and participation into leadership and organizational life.

It seems to have gone largely unnoticed in all of our grasping for enduring leadership approaches that we have examples of leadership in practice that have endured for centuries—millennia, even. Granted, for the most part, these servant leaders of antiquity did not lead great armies or complex organizations, but were often solitary individuals teaching principally through example, through giving of themselves in service. Fortunately, most had a great deal to say—or more accurately, a great deal has been written about what they said. If we assume that the mark of great leadership is lasting influence, the greatest leaders of the ages have been the founders of the enduring religious and philosophical traditions, with hundreds of millions shaping their thoughts and lives around the teachings and examples of this small band of sages. With few exceptions, we find in each of these individuals the finest attributes of service-centered leadership. In some cases—Confucius, for example—there is considerable evidence that he wrote at least a portion of what is attributed to him. Others, such as the Taoist philosopher Lao Tzu, may have been mythical, and known historical figures such as Jesus and Gautama (the Buddha) are best known through the writings of their followers. Each exemplified leadership as service in both principle and practice, and their approaches were sufficiently varied as to give us a full spectrum of examples of enduring, service-based leadership.

Their teachings are occasionally referred to as the Wisdom Literature, and for good reason. Each provides proverbial pearls of great worth which, strung together, create a necklace of counsel and thoughtful instruction for the leader who chooses the path of service. Before discussing the more practical attributes and applications of syncretic leadership, it is worth reviewing the contribution of these great thinkers to the art and practice of leadership—not to make judgments about the relative merit of their philosophies, but to establish those teachings as the inspiration for later servant-leader theory.

THE WISDOM OF THE ORIENT

The Chinese philosopher Confucius was the wisdom philosopher with perhaps the greatest conscious concern for the application of his teachings to secular leadership and governance. To Confucius, born in the seventh century B.C.E. in China's Lu Province, much of his country's former greatness had been lost as the people of his time drifted away from the traditions that had once served as social glue during China's Golden Age. Confucius found in the five Chinese Classics, most notably the I Ching, evidence that in the times of the early dynasties, harmony resulted from complete understanding of, and adherence to, traditional sets of formal relationships. To this teacher, leader, and scholar, the lost harmony and productivity could be restored only through reestablishing those traditions, or in cases in which they could not be restored, creating new deliberate traditions to refocus personal relationships and responsibilities.

Central to Confucian thinking was the concept of li, which is variously translated as "propriety," "proper comportment," and "ritual." He believed that by repeatedly behaving in proper and appropriate ways, we become that way—something of the reverse of the Biblical injunction, "As a man thinketh in his heart, so is he."[2] For Confucius, if a person acted and responded to others in a caring, compassionate, and appreciative way, he or she became caring, compassionate, and appreciative—and at least if failing to do so, created an atmosphere of care, compassion, and concern. Through his teachings, Confucius attempted to develop a complete and careful description of how we should behave as a prelude to beginning to think as we should think—thereby becoming what we should become.

The principle of *li* teaches:

> When you find wealth within your reach, do not get it by improper means; when you meet with calamity, do not escape from it by improper means. Do not seek for victory in small contentions; do not seek for more than your proper share. Do not positively affirm what you have doubts about; and do not let what you say appear (simply) as your own view....One should not please others in an improper way, not be lavish of his words.... To cultivate one's person and fulfill one's words is called good conduct. When the conduct is ordered, and the words are accordant with the course, we have the substance of the rules of *li*.[3]

Confucius refers to the person who fully adheres to the principle of *li* as *chun-tzu*, the superior, noble, or fully human individual. Much of his writing is dedicated to describing this leader. To Confucius, *chun-tzu* (the noble person):

> ...does not accept people because of what they say, nor reject sayings because the speaker is what he is.
> ...is calm and at ease; the small person is fretful and ill at ease.
> ...does not grieve that other people do not recognize his merits. His only anxiety is lest he should fail to recognize theirs.
> ...is ashamed to let his words outrun his deeds.
> ...takes as much trouble to discover what is right as lesser people take to discover what will pay.
> ...calls attention to the good points in others; he does not call attention to their defects. The small person does just the reverse of this.[4]

Though the sayings are simple, the influence has been profound. Every Chinese child is weaned on Confucian principles, and the teachings of Master Kung Fu-Tzu remain the single most powerful shaping influence on Chinese thought and action. The leader in Western society would also be well served to study the principles of *chun-tzu*, *li*, and other Confucian concepts of right action and right thought. Much of the spirit of service-centered leadership is found in them.

Confucius's nemeses, in many ways, were the Taoists, whose philosophy appeared to represent the antithesis of Confucian formalism. Yet its objectives were the same—to seek a means through which universal harmony might be restored. There is within Taoism (*Tao* simply meaning "The Way" or "The Way of the Universe") a wisdom that also informs and inspires the service-centered leader. Its brief 81 verses are so thought provoking that this small text has served as the basis for complete works on leadership—John Heider's *The Tao of Leadership* being a case in point. For our purposes here, a much less complete review of selected Taoist principles will serve to demonstrate their application to leadership in general, and to service-based leadership in particular.

At the heart of Taoist philosophy is the belief that, left to its own devices, the universe would exhibit a full, complete, and natural harmony. It is a harmony created by the perfect balance and commingling of the two vital forces in nature: *yin* and *yang*. When there is disharmony, it is a reflection of this balance being disturbed, usually by human action and intervention. The principal responsibility of human beings then becomes one of living so as to keep activity as closely in harmony with the natural rhythms of nature as possible.

Some mistake this Taoist view as advocating inactivity, but I think it more accurately describes Taoists as embracing harmonious action that is effortless *because* of that harmony.

> One may move so well that a footprint never shows,
> Speak so well that the tongue never slips,
> Reckon so well that no counter is needed,
> Seal an entrance so tight, though using no lock,
> That it cannot be opened,
> Bind a hold so firm, though using no cord,
> That it cannot be untied.
> And these are traits not only of sound man
> But of many a man thought to be unsound.
> A sound man is good at salvage,
> At seeing that nothing is lost.
> Having what is called insight,
> A good man, before he can help a bad man,
> Finds in himself the matter with the bad man.
> And whichever teacher discounts the lesson
> Is as far off the road as the other,
> Whatever else he may know.
> This is the heart of it.[5]

Water is a commonly used metaphor in the *Tao Te Ching* and in other Taoist writings, used because it embodies smoothness and effortlessness, but at the same time, thoroughness, power, and effectiveness. In many ways it exemplifies the effective leader.

> As the soft yield of water cleaves the obstinate stone,
> So to yield with life, solves the insoluble:
> To yield, I have learned, is to come back again.
> But this unworded lesson,
> This easy example,
> Is lost upon men.[6]

The Taoists also understand the importance of leaving some things undone—a lesson occasionally lost on those charged with leadership. There often is value, they observe, in what is absent rather than in what is present.

> Thirty spokes are made one by holes in the hub,
> By vacancies joining them for a wheel's use;
> The use of clay in molding pitchers
> Comes from the hollow of its absence;
> Doors, windows, in a house,
> Are used for their emptiness:
> Thus we are helped by what is not
> To use what is.[7]

This reminder that "we are helped by what is not" brings to mind Jim Collins's observation in *Built to Last* that one of the greatest challenges for many organizations, particularly educational institutions, is to determine what they should *not* be doing—what is *not* part of their mission.[8]

It is through this circumspect seeking of harmony, power in persistent calmness, and value in empty spaces and unspoken words that the Taoists make their most significant contribution to leadership theory in general, and most particularly, to leadership as service. Within Taoism, the leader has importance only through what is accomplished, how it is accomplished, and how others benefit from it.

> A leader is best
> When people barely know that he exists,
> Not so good when people obey and acclaim him,
> Worst when they despise him.
> 'Fail to honor people,
> They fail to honor you;'
> But of a good leader, who talks little,
> When his work is done, his aim fulfilled,
> They will all say, "We did this ourselves."[9]

Considerable attention is given here to the Chinese philosophers, in part, because leadership was a theme for them, and partly because they are theologically less sensitive than others of the Wisdom writers. But the ancients whose teachings were more "theological" still bear at least brief mention since they are our most enduring examples of service-based leadership, and selected teachings offer significant insight into its principles.

THE EIGHTFOLD PATH

In contrast to the pragmatic worldliness of the oriental philosophers, the Buddha advocated complete separation from the things of this world—a position that on its surface would seem to have little to offer today's down-in-the-thick-of-it leader. But Indian philosophy, as ancient as any religious tradition still in practice, provides some of the most profound observations on intellectual development and mental and emotional control to be found in written history. Perhaps this in part explains the growing interest in Buddhism in the West.

Born Siddhartha Gautama to a noble Indian family some six centuries B.C.E., Gautama was wrenched from a life of protected luxury and innocence by unexpected exposure to aging, sickness, and death. By tradition, it was prophesied at his birth that he would become either a great prince or a great holy man. His father, wanting the former, lavished him with the luxuries of life and protected him from any unpleasantness. The gods, knowing that his destiny was as a sage, engineered a series of experiences that touched Gautama to the core and redirected him toward a search for life's meaning. These disturbing revelations eventually resulted in a visionary experience through which he became "The Enlightened One," or The Buddha. Through this experience, he came to believe that all is impermanence, including existence itself, and that seeking permanence in a universe of impermanence creates suffering. At the heart of Buddhist teaching are The Four Noble Truths: that life is suffering, that suffering results from desire (from "wanting"), that suffering can be eliminated if desire is eliminated, and that desire can be quenched by following the "Eightfold Path."

There is an inclination for Westerners to view Buddhism as essentially pessimistic, partly because of a quest for personal extinguishment that the highly individualistic West finds uncomfortable, and partly because we are such a "desires" based society. We find little particularly admirable in the Buddha's advice, "Do not take a liking to anything, for loss of what is liked is bad. There are no fetters for those who have no likes or dislikes."[10] Our purpose here, however, is not to judge the philosophy, but to see what it offers that has value to inspired leadership.

It is in his expositions on the Eightfold Path that the Buddha contributes his most significant thought to leadership. The Eightfold Path is designed to aid the devout seeker with cessation of desire through right views, right intentions, right speech, right action, right livelihood, right effort, right mindedness, and right concentration. From elaboration on these principles, we receive such wisdom as the Buddhist counsel to live in the present, since anger comes from living in the past, and fear from living in the future. Right mindedness, the Buddha taught, was cultivated by developing four qualities: compassion, loving kindness, sympathetic joy, and equanimity.[11] Leaders such as Gandhi, though drawing more specifically from the Hindu and Jain traditions in India, found great leadership strength through the exercise of these attributes of right mindedness.

SERVICE IN THE WESTERN TRADITION

In the West, most of us are more familiar with the teachings and traditions of the great monotheistic religions as presented by their servant leaders, the prophets of Israel, Jesus, and Muhammad. It is interesting, nonetheless, that we often have chosen to ignore their basic principles of leadership and management, more inclined to seek in their teachings support for our personal "desires"—those cravings that were of such concern to the Buddha.

Robert Greenleaf found in the account of the Mosaic organization of the Children of Israel in the wilderness the beginnings of our "top-down" organizational model. Yet it can also be argued that the counsel given by the Hebrew God through Moses began to establish the Western standard for compassion and personal integrity.

"When you reap the harvest of your land," the God of Israel tells Moses, "you shall not reap all the way to the edges of your field, or gather the gleanings of your harvest."[12] The Israelites were not to pick their orchards bare or gather fallen fruit, but were to leave these for the poor and the stranger. The Mosaic books of the Pentateuch instruct the people to return an enemy's wandering ox and assist in raising it if it has fallen. They counsel that one render all judgments fairly, no matter who is concerned, and pay the wages of the laborer before the day ends.[13]

Like the discourses of the Buddha, the teachings of the Christian messiah, Jesus, are concerned primarily with eternal rather than temporal consequences, and earthly leadership and office had little appeal to him. But his own world-shaping leadership was one of complete service, and he encouraged the same in those who followed him. "Let him who will be greatest among you be your servant,"[14] he declared, instructing his followers in all of their activities to be humble, gentle-spirited, forgiving, long-suffering, and peacemakers.

The Muslim prophet, Muhammad, more willingly assumed public leadership, but declared, as a conduit for the words of Allah, that virtue lies only in him who enjoins charity, kindness, and peace among men. Through Muhammad, Allah counseled that if a man be brought a piece of news, he first inquire into its truth, lest he wrong others unwittingly through passing it along falsely. The good person, the Koran instructs, curbs his anger and forgives his fellow man.[15] The Koran is so clearly against the practice of usury that Shariah, Islamic law, prohibits the taking of interest. Fairness and charity govern all human relationships.

I suspect that many reading this chapter have chuckled at the thought of leadership modeled after the service-centered approaches of religious and philosophical traditions. How, one might ask, can a leadership practice based on caring, compassion, selflessness, and integrity survive in the rough and tumble climate of today's business or academic world? Like a Zen koan, the answer lies in contemplating the question. What has endured? What leaders of several millennia ago are still revered, still widely followed? Can we think of *any* who were not servant leaders? What is it that dedicates individuals to commitment? It is belief that what they are doing fulfills some deep personal need and desire, that their lives contribute to a greater good, and matter in some significant way.

Ah, yes! But these teachers promised eternal reward, not just the satisfaction of being helpful while muddling along through mortality! Not always. Confucius and Lao Tzu promised only harmony; the Buddha only personal release from suffering. They have endured as leaders because they provided fulfillment and meaning in life … and what other enduring reason is there to lead, if not to that end?

NOTES

1. Marshall McLuhan, *The Global Village: Transformations in World Life and Media in the Twenty-first Century* (Oxford, England: Oxford University Press, 1989).

2. 23:7 Proverbs KJV.

3. Philip Novak, *The World's Wisdom* (San Francisco: HarperCollins, 1994), 122–123, quoting James Legge, trans., *The Sacred Books of China: The Texts of Confucianism III: The Li Ki* (Oxford, England: Clarendon Press, 1885), 61–89.

4. Ibid., 129, citing Arthur Waley, trans., *The Analects of Confucius* (New York: Random House, 1938).

5. Lao Tzu, *The Way of Life*, trans. Witter Bynner (New York: Putnam, 1972), 56.

6. Ibid., 73.

7. Ibid., 39.

8. James C. Collins and Jerry Porras, *Built to Last: Successful Habits of Visionary Companies* (New York: HarperBusiness, 1994), 165.

9. Lao Tzu, 46.

10. *Dhammapada: The Sayings of the Buddha*, trans. Thomas Cleary (New York: Bantam Books, 1995), 74.

11. Novak, 65–77.

12. Ibid., 188. citing Lev. 19:9–10 NRSV.

13. Ibid., 189–190.

14. Mat. 23:11 NRSV.

15. Novak, 301–308, citing N. J. Dawood, trans., *The Koran* (London: Penguin, 1956).

CHAPTER 4

Shaping a Syncretic Leadership

I do wish that when a principle has been worked out in ethics, it did not have to be discovered all over again in psychology, in economics, in government, in business, in biology, in sociology. It's such a waste of time.
—Mary Parker Follett

I t should not be surprising that the principles of service-centered leadership that proved to be so successful and enduring in the spiritual realm found their way into other areas of leadership at key points in our history. Warren Bennis notes in *Why Leaders Can't Lead* that when the Constitution of the United States was being crafted, half a dozen figures of historical renown contributed to the document—six in a population of only three million citizens.[1]

Bennis observes, however, that it is difficult to identify half that many among a population of nearly 300 million today. On a worldwide basis, we still find that occasional exception—Gandhi, Mother Teresa, and Martin Luther King, Jr., for example—but it is worth noting that these examples have emerged through sociopolitical movements, those movements that bridge the spiritual and the secular. All three recognized the power of service as a catalyst to action, and of placing the dreams and desires of those being led above or beside their own. Each understood that when people believe in the rightness of the vision, they will go to any extreme to bring it to fruition.

Robert Greenleaf found in the life of the eighteenth century humanitarian and journalist John Woolman what he considered to be an ideal in the exercise of Servant-Leadership principles.[2] Woolman was a Quaker who determined that his personal calling was to rid the Quaker community of the evils of slavery. In the early and mid-seventeen hundreds, the Quakers in colonial America were a prosperous, slaveholding people. Yet by 1770, slave ownership had completely disappeared from the Society of Friends, due largely to the work of John Woolman. For 30 years, he traveled the eastern seaboard visiting family after family, discussing the immorality of slavery and demonstrating his empathy for, and understanding of, the needs and desires of both slaveholder and slave. At the core of his message was the moral imperative for the slave owner: "What does slaveholding do to you, as a person? What kind of moral institution are you binding over to your children?" Though Woolman was not a leader of designated position, his influence on the Quaker community was perhaps as profound as was that of any public, religious, or political figure of the time.[3]

It is a challenge to think of a single leader of that caliber in America today. On the world stage, there are several—Nelson Mandela being one. But where are the world-shaping leaders in business? In higher education? The difference, Bennis notes, is that these examples from our historic past were people of commitment to nation and citizenry rather than to money and self, while in both public and private sectors, the so-called leaders of today "confuse quantity for quality and substitute ambition for imagination."[4]

THE MANAGEMENT REVOLUTION

Despite Bennis's expressed cynicism, principles of service-centered leadership are reemerging in the business community, and several of these principles have become mainstays of modern management practice. The management revolution of the 1970s and 80s, championed by Drucker, Deming, and Bennis, among others, recognized that the male-dominated hierarchical organizations of the first seven decades of the twentieth century were inefficient, conflict ridden, driven by greed, and incongruous with the emerging belief that business is a social organization. As such, business, as well as other social institutions, has a responsibility to add to the development of a civil society. Peter Drucker notes about this revolution:

> Now we know that modern organizations have to be built on making conflict constructive—all the more so as the tensions and conflicts and differences are no longer primarily between capital and labor but within a knowledge organization.... We know that ours is a society of organizations and that each organization—and not only a business—is a *social* organization. We know that management has to be a discipline. And we know that just as the concern of the cabinetmaker is the complete sideboard rather than hammer and pliers and screwdriver, the object and concern of management is the entire organization rather than tools and techniques. Finally, we know that restoring citizenship is the crucial challenge. If one lesson was taught by the collapse of the ultimate mega-state, totalitarian communism, it is that nothing can work unless it is based on a functioning civil society—that is, on citizens and citizenship.[5]

This is not to suggest that Drucker and other late twentieth-century management gurus completely embraced Greenleaf's servant-leader principles outlined in Chapter 2. In fact, Greenleaf and Drucker were well acquainted and agreed that they didn't fully see eye to eye. Drucker wrote of Greenleaf, "Bob was always out to change the individual, to make him or her into a different person. I was interested in making people *do* the right things, in their actions and behaviors. Bob was interested in motives; I was interested in consequences."[6] Drucker concedes, however, that he is "probably as much a moralist as Bob was and he (Greenleaf) may have been as much a pragmatist as I am."[7] Whether in full agreement or not, it is apparent from the writings of both that each saw the modern organization as an organic creature, ever changing and evolving, always dependent upon the proper functioning and involvement of each part to make the whole complete. Each also agreed that primary among the responsibilities of leadership are shaping the vision that directs that change, fully involving those within the organization in pursuit of common organizational goals, and structuring those goals so that they contribute to the betterment of society as a whole. This, in and of itself, is a dramatic and heartening movement back toward the altruism of our great leaders of the past.

THE FOLLETT PRINCIPLES

Drucker introduced me to another student of leadership and organizational development who might be viewed as the mother of modern management and leadership theory: Mary Parker Follett. In the introduction to a collection of Follett's writings, Drucker credits Follett with having "struck every single chord in what now constitutes the 'management symphony.'"[8] It is in the writings of Mary Follett that I find the pragmatic application principles for Servant-Leadership that are often missing in much of Greenleaf's writings—applications that create a synergy resulting in the more pragmatic approach to service-centered leadership I call syncretic.

Follett was born in 1868 in Massachusetts, educated in economics, government, law, and philosophy at Radcliff and at Newnham College in Cambridge, England, and spent her early professional life in social work. Her labor as a social worker involved her in the organization and management of homes for troubled children, immersing her in the very practical elements of organizational behavior. This experience and a keen understanding of human nature directed Follett's interests toward a study of organizational dynamics, group processes, and shared governance, leading to the publication in 1920 of *The New State*. In this work, she advocated the replacement of bureaucratic, hierarchical approaches to governance and management with team-managed organizations in which those participating identified problems and worked toward mutually derived solutions. Though occasionally accused of being socialist, her writing attracted national and international attention in business and industrial circles because of its sensible practicality and the apparent success of her model when applied. She was invited to speak to world business leaders at a series of international management conferences, sharpening her own interest in application of her ideas to industry, and leading to the publication in 1924 of what is generally considered her most important work, *Creative Experience*.[9]

In the introduction to the discussion of Follett's contributions to management mentioned above, Drucker suggests that Follett presented four postulates that have foreshadowed modern leadership and management thinking. These included her concepts: (1) of *creative conflict,* (2) of management as a generic activity with application to all organizations, rather than exclusively to business, (3) of management as a *function* rather than as an assortment of tools, and (4) of the importance of reinventing the citizen within the social organization.[10] We now see postulate two, that management approaches can effectively be applied in all organizations, as a given, so our focus here will be on postulates one, three, and four. In many ways, they were early expressions of what has since emerged as service-centered leadership.

Follett viewed conflicts—or what she preferred to call "differences"—as inevitable developments within an organization. She believed them to serve a useful and constructive purpose by illuminating areas of disagreement or misunderstanding that could then be used to foster consensus. She placed great emphasis on what she labeled "The Law of the Situation," arguing that "when there is identification with organizational goals, the members tend to perceive what the situation requires and do it whether the boss exerts influence to have it done or not."[11] Conflict arises when one of two situations exists: employees do not identify with organizational goals, or these goals are differently perceived and understood by employees and the leadership. In either case, the conflict becomes an opportunity to identify which of these deficiencies exists. When resolution of the conflict is approached objectively (Follett liked to say "scientifically"), the result can be a creatively "integrated" solution that strengthens the organization and serves all concerned.

The Law of the Situation dictates that when carefully and honestly examined, the facts of a situation contain the solution within them.[12] Key to finding this solution is complete candor and openness among those involved in the conflict, plus the opportunity for as many as possible to thoroughly examine the problem. Though the solution may exist in the problem, it will not be readily apparent to everyone, and the more who examine it, the more likely one of those involved will see the best solution. This broad involvement introduces a second part of Follett's Creative Conflict principle—the concept of *power-with* rather than *power-over.*

"No word is used more carelessly by us all than the word 'power,'" Follett claimed, arguing that in most cases we use it in reference to power-over.[13] Power-over is the power of position, of coercion, of manipulation by an entity or individual to bend another to the first's will. Power-with, by contrast, is integrative, considering the desires of all concerned in finding solutions. It assumes that the collective we has the power to satisfy all or most of our desires through serious examination of our interests, with specific attention given to where they appear to be in conflict. If both parties adhere to The Law of the Situation, Follett maintained, neither has power over the other, but both find power within the situation to identify mutually advantageous solutions. She wrote:

> If your business is so organized that you can influence a co-manager while he is influencing you, so organized that a workman has an opportunity of influencing you as you have of influencing him: if there is an interactive influencing going on all the time between you, power-with may be built up.[14]

Conflict, when handled in this objective way, begins to serve as a vital, creative force within the organization. The first rule for obtaining integration, Follett suggested, was that you must "put your cards on the table, face the real issue, uncover the conflict, bring the whole thing into the open."[15] To do so requires remarkable internal trust, a trust that, along with the concept of power-with and its integrating result, closely parallels the Servant-Leadership precepts of Greenleaf, but adds to them a syncretic practicality.

It is a trust that some do not see as possible. Nitin Nohria, in a commentary on Follett's writing, observed: "Trust, as others wiser than I have noted, is a fragile thing. It is hard to build and easy to destroy. All it takes to destroy trust is a few people who are driven to acquire power-over as opposed to power-with."[16] Anyone with much organizational experience knows that Nohria is right, but this does not make the integrating nature of Follett's power-with less desirable. It simply demands that a critical role of the leader is to find those particular points of conflict and help the individuals involved recognize that there can be a win-win with shared power—which provides a nice segue to the third postulate listed by Drucker, that management (and here I will include leadership) is a "function" within an organization, rather than a group of tools to facilitate power-over.

Follett, in her writing, directly addressed the issue of "service," but chose to substitute the word "function." Speaking of "service," she stated: "I do not wholly like the present use of that word…. This word is often used sentimentally, or at least vaguely, to express good intentions, or even, like charity, to cover a multitude of sins."[17] In a paper originally titled "How must Business Managers Develop in Order to Become a Profession?" she explained that her concern with use of the word "service" was that she saw people who regularly made money during the day for purely selfish reasons, often to the detriment of those with whom they worked, justify themselves in the evenings by providing "service" to their communities through civic activity. "The much more wholesome idea, which we have now," she states, "is that our work itself is to be our greatest service to the community."[18] When service is thought of as "reciprocal," as connoting an exchange of assistance within the workplace, she found use of the word more acceptable but still preferred "function" since it contributed more fully to the organic metaphor she applied to the organization.

In Follett's model organization, each person, from the leader to the line worker, contributes some vital function without which the organization cannot be wholly effective. Some responsibilities require broader scope and understanding, but if the organization is complete without being redundant, none is nonessential. As with physiological organisms, the organization cannot be totally effective if any part is missing or functions inadequately, and the responsibility of each part extends beyond mere service to other functions. Each must view itself as a *vital* organ, with the existence and survival of the organization dependent upon every function working in a healthy and coordinated way. With this view of integrated service, the principle of power-with becomes much clearer and organizationally important.

Those with even brief college leadership experience have seen this principle in action. Who is missed more when away from the campus? The president, or the switchboard operator? On a day-to-day basis, who routinely provides the more vital function? The president, or the computer tech who keep the college's information system up and running smoothly? We know that each role is vital, but we often fail to recognize that essential nature by involving these personnel in power-sharing.

The last of Follett's organizational postulates mentioned by Drucker is the need to reinvent the citizen within the organization. Follett sees a constant interplay of action and ideals. Ideals should, in her mind, guide our actions, and actions will in the process inform our ideals. I am reminded here of the circular Confucian concept that "structured behavior" can demonstrate the value of the social ideals that underpin the behavior, leading to a unity of the whole. Through this interplay of action and ideals, Follett believed we come to understand the value of a system of ethics that can guide organizational and individual behavior.[19]

"We do not follow right, we create right," Follett argued. Lest this be understood as a completely situational ethic, it must be explained that she meant by this that our sense of right must be constantly engaged, constantly in the present. Ethics are not a collection of ornaments we tuck away on a shelf, to be pulled out and displayed when we face what we perceive to be an ethical dilemma. "The ideal which is to be used for our life must come out from that very life itself," she said. "The only way our past ideals can help us is in molding the life which produces the present ideal.... But we do not discard them: we have built them into the present—we have used them up as the cocoon is used up in making the silk."

Organizations, in much the same way, develop a collective morality—an understanding of what is right based on the coming together in the present of the dynamic ideals of all involved. This collective sense of right generates an organizational conscience, a group understanding of what is best for the organization and for all involved with it. From this interrelated understanding of right comes a common sense of purpose—the basis for organizational commitment and loyalty.[20] When the organization is the larger community, the result is an informed and committed citizen, loyal not by coercion or force, but by an established trust that shared ideals will guide collective action. Follett offers a succinct summation of her thinking by observing: "Leaders and followers are both following the invisible leader—the common purpose."[21]

As with Greenleaf, there is an unabashed idealism in Follett that some view as impractical. Much of the world of modern management thought does not. As mentioned earlier, Drucker credits Follett with having struck every major chord in the modern management symphony. In 1986, Tokihiko Enomoto, professor of business administration at Tokai University in Japan, established the Mary Parker

Follett Association of Japan and, with a colleague, published a study of Follett's life. He credits much of the management revolution in Japan to the writings of Chester Barnard and his principle of cooperation as the basis for effective organization. Enomoto notes that in their study of Barnard, they found frequent reference to Follett's work, and directed new attention to her writing. "Little by little, Follett's work has become part of our teaching on management and is well known to quite a number of our mid- and upper-level managers who staff our government institutions and business organizations," he observes.[22]

Other admiring students include Bennis who, as founder of the Leadership Institute at the University of Southern California, remembers Follett as a cult figure during his formative years.[23] Sir Peter Parker, who served as chairman of the London School of Economics until late 1998, said of Follett, "She has mattered more to me than any other of the founders of modern management this century."[24] Of Follett, Rosabeth Moss Kanter wrote: "We should all stand on Follett's shoulders in order to see further into the possibilities of organizational perfection."[25]

Why, one might ask, was Follett such a sensation in the early decades of the 1900s, but virtually disappeared as an influence for half a century? Some suggest that it was because she was a woman, and the business and industrial world was not yet prepared to be guided by a woman's insights. Others speculate that the depression of the late 1920s and early 1930s left many feeling powerless and anxious to turn their fates over to authoritarian figures who promised to help them out of their dismal situations. Perhaps her ideas were simply too far ahead of their time, and needed the better part of a century to percolate and find a more receptive organizational climate.

To our good fortune, she has been rediscovered and provides a perfect partner for the idealist Greenleaf. Her concepts of creative conflict, the Law of the Situation and power-with, infuse a sense of "how," into Greenleaf's more idealized "what should be." Her observations are consistent with my experience—that if the organization is efficiently designed, each individual is critical to its successful functioning and each is as entitled to "want from it" as is the leader.

As we turn now to the more practical applications of syncretic leadership in the academic world, I will constantly be returning to both Greenleaf and Follett as the foundational figures upon whom rests much of what I see as critical to good leadership. Both believed that, to paraphrase Greenleaf, for anything great to happen within an organization, there must first be a vision, a clear sense of what can and should be. It is to creating that vision that we now turn our attention.

NOTES

1. Warren Bennis, *Why Leaders Can't Lead* (San Francisco: Jossey-Bass, 1989), 33.

2. Robert K. Greenleaf, *On Becoming a Servant Leader*, ed. Don M. Frick and Larry Spears (San Francisco: Jossey-Bass, 1996), 290–291.

3. John Woolman, *The Journal of John Woolman*, ed. Janet Whitney (Kila, MT: Kessinger, 2006).

4. Bennis, 33.

5. Peter F. Drucker, introduction to *Mary Parker Follett: Prophet of Management*, by Pauline Graham, ed. (Boston: Harvard Business School Press, 1995), 8.

6. Peter F. Drucker, foreword to *On Becoming a Servant Leader*, by Don M. Frick and Larry Spears, ed. (San Francisco: Jossey-Bass, 1996), xi–xii.

7. Ibid., xi–xii.

8. Drucker, *Mary Parker Follett*, 2.

9. Mary Parker Follett, *Mary Parker Follett: Prophet of Management*, ed. Pauline Graham (Boston: Harvard Business School Press, 1995), 16–17.

10. Ibid., 4–8.

11. Mary Parker Follett, *Dynamic Administration: The Collected Papers of Mary Parker Follett*, ed. Elliot M. Fox and L. Urwick (London: Pitman, 1973), 31.

12. Follett, *Prophet of Management*, 107.

13. Follett, *Dynamic Administration*, 67.

14. Follett, *Prophet of Management*, 107.

15. Ibid., 75.

16. Ibid., 160–161.

17. Follett, *Dynamic Administration*, 103.

18. Ibid., 104.

19. Follett, *Prophet of Management*, 248–254.

20. Ibid., 248–254.

21. Mary Parker Follett, *Freedom & Co-ordination: Lectures in Business Organization by Mary Parker Follett*, ed. L. Urwick (London: Management Publications Trust, 1949), 56.

22. Follett, *Prophet of Management*, 242.

23. Ibid., 177

24. Ibid., 282.

25. Ibid., xviii.

CHAPTER

Shaping the Vision

Not much happens without a dream. Behind every great achievement is
a dreamer of great dreams. Much more than a dream is needed to bring
it to reality; but the dream must be there first.

—Robert K. Greenleaf

To say that higher education in America is without vision would be both
inaccurate and unfair—at least if vision refers to some expressed sense of
what an institution wants to become and what it will take to get there.
The pervasive flaw in the American academic community is that its visionary
focus remains too completely on the functions institutions wish to perform rather
than on what best serves students and others who should benefit, if vision were
extended.

The criticisms raised by Frank Newman's Futures Project mentioned in Chapter
1—that there is a "growing gap between the public's needs and the performance
of colleges and universities"[1] in an array of critical service areas—suggest that
we are either suffering from severe tunnel vision, or we have lost the capacity or
courage to move in the direction indicated by a broader vision. To list once more
the Futures Project's concerns in simple terms, we are failing to teach as well as
we should, to support students effectively through the learning process, to use our
resources productively, and to strengthen and support other segments of formal
education. We allow conflicts of interest to shape our research agendas, muffle the
voices of social criticism within our ranks, and are disengaged from the process of
sustaining our democratic system. These indictments are both broad and severe,
yet other thoughtful critics echo Newman's concerns.

Milton Greenberg observes that, "Still missing from most faculty preparation and professional development is the place of higher education in the nation and the world, the underlying and pervasive social issues that affect it, and the great potential power of academic citizenship."[2] Greenberg attributes this deficiency to:

> the academy's well-honed sense of dread at the idea that higher education is part of the world at all. One of the academy's core values is institutional autonomy, treasured as an enclave free of political and economic concerns. In many cases, faculty members can barely see beyond their own discipline or narrow specialization, viewing even that as independent of their own campus issues.[3]

This sense of "cloistered existence" by the most powerful and protected voices within the academy not only has had a limiting, but also a stifling effect on how broadly many are willing to define vision. We talk of institutions that value student achievement, serve as social critics, actively engage students, faculty, and the extended community in discussion of critical issues, but both our actions and our measures of success belie these priorities. We continue to evaluate our institutions in terms of the strength of traditional curricula, growth in enrollment, and addition of new buildings. For all but the very elite, growth remains the principal sign of health—growth in enrollment, growth in endowment, growth in number of grants received, and growth in campus facilities. It is the rare college president who isn't annually plagued with the question, "How do the fall numbers look?" Students mean revenue—or at least provide justification for requesting more money—and the only situation that permanently closes college doors is financial insolvency.

Unfortunately, the vast majority of financial closures have been in the private sector, while among publics, weak and unneeded institutions find political constituencies to keep them open, even when it is clearly not in the best interests of the public to do so. These institutions and their more viable partners continue to submit capital budget requests based on aggressive campus expansion, despite stable or declining student numbers and the likelihood that advances in telecommunications technology will make fewer permanent facilities necessary. Building a new structure, needed or not, is seen as energizing a campus, creating a perception among students and the general public that something vital is happening.

One university president whose institution was investing millions in new and renovated facilities explained the value of these investments by suggesting that in addition to attracting students, new buildings and an attractive campus allowed the college to attract more faculty and more distinguished professors. Yet the report that included this rationale also noted that 42 percent of faculty at this university were part-time.[4] Was the vision one of having the best faculty or of having the nicest facilities?

"It's become an arms race," observes Richard Hersh of the Harvard Center for Moral Education. "So you have to have what everybody else has, and what everybody else has, may or may not have anything to do with whether it's good for education."[5]

Vision wears the blinders of the past, and is driven forward under the whip of growth-based appropriations. As with other arms races, we are fully aware that we would be better off committing new revenues to supporting the public good (strengthening the academic experience of a relatively fixed number of students,) but we use them instead to expand floor space, beef up recruiting budgets, and add game rooms and food courts to stave off ambushes on the available student pool by other universities.

Yet few of us are able to demonstrate what has happened to our students in terms of their personal development as globally, socially, and politically aware citizens.

We provide little or nothing to the public to indicate what difference their vast investment in grants and research has made, or to account for the productivity of our publicly supported employees. We herald the awarding of major grants, but rarely report to the public on their results. A few major research findings are broadly publicized, but there is no accountability, internally or externally, for the huge public investment that goes into thousands of other studies that might be viewed by the public as meaningless academic exercises.

We know even less about the impact of the institution on the average citizen in the larger community. Is he or she more culturally aware because we exist? Better attuned to the monumental changes that are reshaping our environment, our economic, social, and cultural future? At the university level, we have not, in most cases, viewed it as our role to educate the masses—leaving that to community colleges, then looking down our noses at the fact that they cater to the economically disadvantaged or the undereducated. But what kind of vision is this, if we are failing to see it as part of our responsibility to promote and provide broad-based public education on critical issues?

While clashes of culture have always created tensions, they have never been more apparent on a global scale, nor seemed more intractable. We remain constantly at war with an enemy we don't understand, and there is little public discourse about why these problems exist and what can be done about them. As a nation, we are rapidly yielding to Asia as the world's dominant economy, yet seem puzzled that we are no longer the preeminent manufacturing society, and futilely struggle to correct rather than adjust to it. Demographic data in the United States indicates that we are creating a permanent underclass and will be unable to sustain our social support systems in the foreseeable future. But who is leading public discussion on these issues and offering solutions?

The popular media relentlessly brings these realities into our homes, but offers little in the way of compelling explanation and even less in terms of solutions. The most objective and analytical news sources are accessed by a limited few, with the general public gaining its information in snippets on the nightly news or from local media sources that spend little time engaging in serious public discourse and debate. Politicians refuse to address contentious issues head-on, valuing political futures above the public good.

The one institution in our society that exists to collect, analyze, and objectively dispense public knowledge in all its forms is the university, and its vision must encompass establishing itself as social critic, broad-based public educator, and citizen builder. By broad-based public education, I do not mean monthly lectures in the Student Commons by distinguished professors or the occasional book on the subject, but presentations to church groups, union meetings, high school civics classes, and senior centers. Wherever regular people gather, our best and brightest should be there to share, provoke, and energize.

"RAILROAD" VISION

Granted, these "best and brightest" have other things on their plates, and much of the significant research affecting our lives comes from their work in the academy. Through the past century, their teaching has prepared the professional workforce that built and sustained our dominant economy. But as the last century closed, there was a growing sense in the business world that even here, our vision was becoming shuttered. *Training & Development* magazine reported that, in 1995, employers spent over $55 billion on education and training in the United States—up 20 percent from a decade before.[6] Ronald Compton, chairman of Aetna Life, noted in an article written for *Corporate Board* that: "The pace of change in how we do business is accelerating, as are concerns over the health of our social and educational institutions. As a result, corporations find that they must take responsibility for teaching and training employees."[7] And Robert Lear, former CEO (chief executive officer) of F&M Schaefer, began an article in *Chief Executive* by stating:

> Don't start howling derisively when I say this, but I think the CEO's job at one of today's corporations is beginning to resemble that of the dean at a big business school.
>
> The CEO must decide what will be taught, who will teach, and who will train the teachers. The classrooms are the company plants and offices scattered all over the world. Of course, the students are paid to take the courses, but the competition for good grades is just as intense and the career rewards for the top students as enticing…. To cope with this enormous and growing educational need, an intriguing new technique is gaining momentum. It is the Corporate University. It is Motorola University, Ford University, Harley Davidson University, and Cambrex University.[8]

With few exceptions, our sense of vision has been so limited by traditional academic structure and curricular approaches that we are letting industry redefine what a college education for twenty-first century employment must be, and are allowing the corporate world to usurp the responsibility for delivering it.

Several noted business schools *are* reexamining and rethinking what business education should be about. Penn's Wharton School, The University of Michigan, and Harvard are retooling their curricula or are developing customized options. In 1995, Harvard hired consultants McKinsey and Co. to revamp its business offerings, with the consultant's initial evaluation concluding that many companies were beginning to view what had once been the nation's premier business program as outdated and staffed with "stodgy and arrogant" faculty.[9] Harvard immediately responded and began to retool its programs to reflect a new relevance.

But these are the schools and programs with the greatest direct connectivity with the rest of society, with their fingers directly on the pulse of international markets and economies. There is remarkably little evidence that these same changes are occurring widely in the academy.

Even within institutions at the divisional level, vision is limited to traditional roles and is held captive by the will to survive. Departments muddle along well after they cease to serve any viable purpose, propped up by their own esoteric justifications. Tenured faculty are retained and shuffled around internally, even when they receive abysmal teaching evaluations, are not able to sustain the expected teaching load, and have not produced a single significant piece of research in years. The cloistered nature of the academy is protected, in many instances, to hide these blemishes that we know would never withstand public scrutiny. Standards of good teaching are routinely compromised in the interest of committing additional time to research or to maintaining headcount.

I was a recent witness to a meeting of state academic leaders at which an admission requirement for junior-level acceptance into teacher education was being discussed. The state's higher education governing body had decreed several years earlier that by the date of this particular meeting, all students entering teacher education programs would meet a minimum standard on a nationally normed achievement test prior to their junior year. Yet few of the colleges in attendance were enforcing the requirement. The president of one of the few complying institutions asked why others were ignoring the mandate. She pointed out that this was an achievement requirement for admission to teacher education, not for graduation, and was therefore simply a matter of committing to implement the standard.

"Standardized test scores aren't accurate indicators of student ability to be good teachers," one academic vice president declared.

"The demand for teachers outstrips our student pool, and we need to increase the pool to meet demand," another argued.

It was apparent to even the most uninformed observer that the enrollment viability of each institution's program was at the heart of the discussion—even for the president who had raised the concern. "I'm losing students to those of you who have ignored the standard," she complained. "Why should I be the only one to follow this guideline if it's going to hurt my enrollment?"

Not once during this discussion did anyone suggest that perhaps every university in the state did not need a teacher education program. No one argued that there might be a relationship between the acceptance of teacher education candidates who are not academically strong, public perception of teacher preparation, and public willingness to support better wages for teachers. Vision was being shaped by institutional self-interest based on economic viability rather than by sound academic judgment.

School principals in the same state were complaining that graduate education in School Administration was outdated and out of touch with the realities of today's school environment. At a Principals' Academy, those attending contended that many faculty in university leadership programs had not spent a full day in a public school in decades, and had experienced the monumental changes in student backgrounds and behavior, legal issues, academic expectations, and technological innovation only through articles they had read or, worse yet, written. A superintendent commented that faculty in general understood the world only as it is reflected "in the literature."

"For you people, the world of research," he complained, "is more real than the world I live in every day. And I'm getting an advanced degree from you to better cope with a reality you have never experienced."

There seems an apt metaphor here in the Hindu Sankhya system, a philosophy that acknowledges two states of being: one of pure consciousness (*purusha*), and one of gross matter (*prikriti*). *Prikriti* binds and holds back *purusha*, limiting the soul's ability to experience complete bliss and enlightenment. Life's goal, therefore, becomes one of freeing one's soul from the restricting fetters of the material world. Perhaps we in the academy have created an existential vision that inclines us to believe that, to remain intellectually pure, we must separate ourselves from a defiling world, with the result that we cease to understand it and therefore cannot serve its needs to free its own intellectual capacity.

DEFINING VISION

An amusing and often distressing hobby for some who have been in the higher education business for many years has been to watch what might be labeled "mission-chasing funding." As states shift resource priorities within their educational budgets, two-year colleges suddenly decide they should be four-year institutions, universities discover that they should have a greater technical mission than they had previously considered, including the addition of associate degree programs, and highly selective institutions decide to lighten up on admissions requirements. As state funding priorities change, institutional rhetoric and capital priorities slide from information systems to homeland security support to biotech, with little discernable change in curricula. There is obviously more than a trace of cynicism evident here, but when funding is involved, mission and vision have a way of becoming remarkably flexible, adjustable, and of secondary importance.

Even the mission statements we put in writing generally focus on what a student is likely to get, rather than on what he or she should become. Many describe programmatic offerings and credentials that can be acquired, but say little about what students will know or be able to do when they leave the college. Fewer address the institution's responsibility to those who work within the organization, to those who populate its broader community and support the college financially.

Certainly college leaders must be concerned with enrollment, revenue flow, and breadth of offering. They cannot ignore contractual obligations, the demands of accreditation, legal concerns based on the new consumerism and "implied contract." But is this vision? Vision by its very nature transcends the mundane and pragmatic. It directs us from the actual toward the ideal. It forces us to ask basic questions about why we exist at all, about the nature and value of education in general, and about work and what work should be all about.

While serving as president of the University of Iowa, Hunter Rawlings delivered an address to faculty, quoted briefly in Chapter 1, in which he characterized vision by suggesting that members of the academic community were "a privileged profession," secure in their place of privilege and insulated from the grinding poverty, violence, and abuse that plagued great segments of society. He referenced the endemic greed of the 1980s and the men who symbolized Wall Street run amuck, "driven by the appetites of countless executives willing to engage in fraud, rampant speculation or anything else for easy money." He challenged his colleagues:

> Until we forsake personal aggrandizement and focus our efforts and talents upon the real needs of our society, the problems of poverty and illiteracy can only worsen.
>
> This is the decade when selfishness has to yield to public spiritedness and generosity in our national life. Why not start this decade by emphasizing what we should give, rather than what we should get? This year, why not focus on our obligations, our responsibilities, our commitment to community?[10]

Whether one agrees with Rawlings's philosophically or not, *this* is vision. Vision leaps beyond results to give purpose and moral significance to the effort; to provide meaning. James MacGregor Burns, in his Pulitzer Prize winning classic, *Leadership*, classified leadership that successfully articulates and motivates action based upon shared vision and moral purpose as "transformational."

> The transforming leader recognizes and exploits an existing need or demand of a potential follower. But, beyond that, the transforming leader looks for potential motives in followers, seeking to satisfy higher needs, and engages the full person of the follower. The result of transforming leadership is a relationship of mutual stimulation and elevation that converts followers into leaders and may convert leaders into moral agents.[11] ... Such leadership occurs when one or more persons engage with others in such a way that leaders and followers raise one another to higher levels of motivation and morality. Their purposes, which might have started out as separate, but related ... become fused.... Power bases are linked not as counterweights but as mutual support for common purpose. But transformational leadership ultimately becomes moral in that it raises the level of human conduct and ethical aspiration of both the leader and the led, and thus it has a transforming affect on both.[12]

The "Yes, but..." that often accompanies a discussion of visionary leadership is that this kind of leadership requires personal charisma; the presence and poetry of Martin Luther King on the steps of the Lincoln Memorial, of Kennedy at his inauguration, or of Shakespeare's young King Henry on the eve of St. Crispin's. Our image of the delivery is almost synonymous with our memory of the message.

We are less inclined to envision the gaunt, quiet figure of Lincoln standing on the platform above Gettysburg, or the slight, bespectacled Gandhi addressing the All India Conference. Yet the vision of the latter two was no less transformational, assurance that the power of the vision is not in the style of the deliverer, but in the message and in the internal passion, integrity, and conviction with which it is delivered.

Collins notes of his Level 5 leaders that "The good-to-great leaders never wanted to become larger-than-life heroes. They never aspired to be put on a pedestal or become unreachable icons. They were seemly ordinary people quietly pursuing extraordinary results."[13] These are people with vision and with the courage to pursue it.

In a college and university context, a vision based on service must include more than the generic commitment to be all we can be. Though there is wisdom in crafting a brief and memorable "vision statement" that the college community can memorize and use as a foundation for guiding decisions and actions, to become operational, the vision must be defined in clearer and more explicit terms.

Not surprisingly, many of the clearer statements of vision that appear in college bulletins come from the private sector. Milwaukee's Alverno College, led for three decades by Sister Joel Read, who also was actively involved with Robert Greenleaf's foundation, expects its graduates to demonstrate competencies in eight critical abilities, in addition to demonstrated academic achievement. These abilities include communication, analysis, problem solving, valuing in decision-making, social interaction, global perspectives, effective citizenship, and aesthetic responsiveness. The catalog, in addition to defining what each of these abilities means to the Alverno student, declares:

> But as valuable as it is … knowledge is not enough. Woven through all classes are activities that help students advance to successively higher levels of sophistication in each of eight abilities. A science course, for example, helps students develop communication abilities. The eight abilities give backbone to Alverno's curriculum, uniting it with a common purpose for teaching and an organizing framework for learning…. Faculty have defined six levels of sophistication for each of the eight abilities. To graduate, a student must advance to the fourth level in all of them. In addition, every student must fulfill the requirements for a major and a support area. These requirements vary somewhat from department to department, but they generally involve advancing to the fifth or sixth level of competence in those abilities that are most closely related to the student's selected major and support area of study…. Alverno's method of evaluating students, called assessment, helps a student and her teachers judge her command of the subject matter and mastery of the eight abilities. Unlike testing, assessments evaluate not just what the student knows, but how well she can apply what she knows.[14]

Some public institutions have made an attempt at describing student learning expectations in this kind of detail, but often shy away from aspirations that are too subjective or might be construed as advocating certain values. The inclination of regional accrediting bodies to require institutions to demonstrate in quantifiable ways how they are achieving institutional goals inclines us to view subjective criteria as liabilities in accreditation reviews. How do we demonstrate, for example, that we are equipping students to live lives that are more ethically and aesthetically rewarding? Nevertheless, in creating vision, the service-centered leader has a responsibility to reinfuse institutional mission with discussion of values. Central to a well-rounded education is the essential need to equip students with the understandings, experiences, and ethical tools required to grapple with the truly monumental issues that will be central to improving the human condition during the students' lifetimes. Without discussion of values, there can be no discussion of purpose, of meaning, or of the reasons to be of service. If accrediting bodies want quantifiable results, we must find ways to provide them rather than avoid the challenges that might make producing them more difficult. A primary responsibility of the syncretic leader is to help all served by the institution find, through the actions and activities of the organization, greater personal sense of purpose and greater desire to be of service—and these objectives must be clear in the institution's statement of vision.

VISION AND VALUES

Rushworth Kidder argues convincingly that there *are* values that virtually all humans hold in common, what he refers to as "core values." In *Shared Values for a Troubled World: Conversations with Men and Women of Conscience*, Kidder reports the results of a very modest but pointed survey of 24 individuals from various cultures and backgrounds, all of whom he judged to represent ethical thinking in the minds of their peers. He found that a common list of values emerged from the interviews, including *love, truth, fairness, freedom, unity, tolerance, responsibility*, and *respect for life*.[15] In the ethics workshops conducted by the Kidder Institute worldwide, this survey is administered to participants with surprisingly similar results. People the world over agree that there are values common to all societies.

Leaders committed to service must embrace these intrinsic human values. For those in education, building persons of integrity, persons committed to caring for others, men and women who are tolerant and can work cooperatively, and citizens who view and judge the world from a position of informed reason must be as much a part of our vision as is fostering intellectual curiosity and creative genius. Otherwise, we build a world of phenomenal invention and wonderful technology, but without the heart and soul to make its use rational and worthwhile.

In many cases, creating and articulating this vision will not be heralded with shouts of acclamation, even within our own organizations. Creating a vision based on personal growth and caring and an expanded sense of the institution's social responsibility often will not be heralded at all, but will be met with considerable resistance. Greenleaf noted that we are not likely to become more caring until our society becomes less power-ridden, and even the dynamics of the university community continue to be based upon power. Control, protection, influence, and coercion remain mainstays of internal relationships. But leadership is about change and movement. If change is not a necessity, all a college requires is a manager—someone to monitor the gauges and stay the course. Leaders chart a new course, and the service-centered leader charts a course with a vision toward greater human involvement, understanding, and goodness.

In the fireside chat with Peter Vaill mentioned earlier, he observed that creating vision is akin in some ways to embarking upon a journey of exploration. It is exploration because we do not have a perfect view of what is out there ... only a sense that there are new opportunities over the horizon. We know that there will be dangers, but we proceed anyway because we believe the benefits of new insights and understandings to outweigh the risks. We try to prepare for the journey as well as our limited vision allows, taking with us those who have experience with exploration and who share our passion for discovery. But much of the territory is unexplored.[16]

The responsibility is frightening. Yet most of us, in our heart of hearts, know that it is what we should be about. A quote that is often attributed to Nelson Mandela actually came from Marianne Williamson, but is no less appropriate. She stated, "Our deepest fear is not that we are inadequate. Our deepest fear is that we are powerful beyond measure. It is our light, not our darkness, that most frightens us."[17]

NOTES

1. Frank Newman, Lara Couturier, and Jamie Scurry, "Higher Education Isn't Meeting the Public's Needs," *Chronicle of Higher Education*, 15 October 2004, B6.

2. Milton Greenberg, "The Power of Academic Citizenship," *Chronicle of Higher Education*, 3 February 2006, B20.

3. Ibid.

4. *Declining by Degrees*, DVD, produced by Learning Matters, Inc. (Public Broadcasting Service, 2005).

5. Ibid.

6. Haidee Allerton, "New Numbers," *Training & Development* 50 (1996): 8.

7. Ronald E. Compton, "Re-educating the corporation," *Corporate Board* 14 (1993): 1.

8. Robert Lear, "Rah, rah for new Corporate U." *Chief Executive*, April 1997, 18.

9. Jennifer Reingold, "Corporate America Goes to School," *Business Week*, 20 October 1997, 66.

10. Charles Bullard, "Rawlings: Reject greed and begin era of giving," *Des Moines Register*, 22 August 1990, A10.

11. James MacGregor Burns, *Leadership* (New York: Harper & Row, 1978), 4.

12. Ibid., 20.

13. Jim Collins, *Good to Great* (New York: HarperCollins, 2001), 28.

14. Alverno College, *1996–98 Bulletin* (Milwaukee, WI: Alverno College, 1996), 3–4.

15. Rushworth M. Kidder, *Shared Values in a Troubled World: Conversations with Men and Women of Conscience* (San Francisco: Jossey-Bass, 1994).

16. Peter Vaill, "A Fireside Chat with Peter Vaill," *Peter Vaill Presentation* (Robert K. Greenleaf Center for Servant-Leadership, 1996), audio cassette recording.

17. Marianne Williamson, *A Return to Love* (New York: HarperCollins, 1992), 165.

CHAPTER

Hearing Every Voice

Leadership is a serious meddling in other people's lives.

—Max De Pree

The preceding chapters have been groundwork, discussion of the philosophies that underlie this syncretic leadership approach and justify the need
for broader vision and new leadership dynamics. If all that was required
of service-centered leadership was a change in attitude about responsibility, we
could wrap it up here with a "Go, and do thou likewise."[1] And I have met college administrators with considerable experience with the principles of Greenleaf's Servant-Leadership who believed exactly that—that if a leader simply
decides he or she is service-oriented, the result will be a more caring and serving
organization. I also know of a colleague who was thoroughly immersed in the
Servant-Leadership philosophy—who saw himself as a servant-leader —but was
forced from office after a faculty vote of "no confidence." He was, according
to those he worked with, autocratic, dictatorial, and completely unwilling to
consider suggestions from others about how the institution could be improved.
His situation illustrates that there is much more to service-based leadership than
Captain Picard's declaration, "Make it so."[2]

If the fundamental principle of syncretic leadership is to help each person
served by the organization realize personal goals of growth and service, while
at the same time furthering the mission of the institution in an atmosphere of
power-with, the leader's first responsibility must be to learn what those goals are.
In an organization of any size, and with constituencies that extend well beyond
the campus, this is no small task.

Several decades ago, "Management by Walking Around" received a great deal of play in organizational circles. The idea was that the leader/manager needed to get out of the office and circulate through the places where people do the work, see what was going on, and ask employees what they thought. The concept still has great value, and with the more broadly participatory approaches to management that followed the Deming revolution, most leaders now spend more time circulating. In fact, Deming is quoted as having said that "If you wait for people to come to you, you'll only get small problems. You must go and find them. The big problems are where people don't realize they have one in the first place."[3]

But universities provide a particular set of challenges for leaders who seek to hear every voice. By structure, tradition, and inclination, the internal voices are muted by a particularly closed system, and many of the important external voices are either intimidated or alienated by the university mystique.

FINDING TIME TO LISTEN

Two problems invariably complicate "walking around" leadership. The first is *time*. As faithfully as many of us try to schedule time to get out and about, travel demands, legislative hearings, appointments with prospective donors, civic responsibilities, and packed meeting schedules make it practically impossible to be seen regularly on all parts of the campus and throughout the community. Large complexes and multicampus organizations add to the constraints of time and to the inability to spread it evenly. Even when time is found to circulate, there are natural traffic patterns—easy places to go—which often miss critical voices altogether. The faculty office building next door is a quick way to see dozens of people in an hour and helps the leader feel "connected" with a fairly brief commitment of time. Down the street, the Physical Plant building is off the beaten path, but houses ten maintenance workers who have never met the president face-to-face, even though the leader feels that he or she gets out regularly. Weekly attendance at the Daybreak Rotary Club does not expose the college president to the Vietnamese immigrant community that has become the region's largest ethnic group, many of whom have no idea who the president is. When some people are seen with regularity and others rarely, walking around may create a sense of favoritism and exclusion rather than one of inclusion and interest.

How does the leader find time for those "not so accessible" constituents? From watching colleagues over the years who did this well and those who did it poorly, I have reached two conclusions: Leaders find time for what they view as important and for what they find personally comfortable. They do *not* find time for what they may know to be important but find uncomfortable, unless it is forced upon them. Some may not enjoy testifying in front of the legislature, but must out of necessity. Getting out and mixing with the quieter, less insistent voices in the college's community may never be presented as a necessity, even if these constituents have some of the greatest needs. Leaders must impose the necessity upon themselves. Those who recognize the value of personal contact with faculty, custodians, and the new Vietnamese immigrant community *and enjoy that contact* find time for it. Those who do not enjoy this contact and cannot develop at least a willingness to do so are probably not suited to lead today's colleges and universities.

Some will argue that one of the reasons leaders have staff is to send these emissaries out to listen to constituent voices. That's what Community Relations offices are for—and provosts and vice presidents. Not if the vision is to be viewed by the college's various publics as the leader's vision. Staff members contribute to and support the vision—but cannot create it whole cloth and articulate it publicly.

Remember the difference in your perception when you were given even five minutes with a congressman or senator during a capital visit rather than with an aide. You left feeling important, cared about, and with a much greater respect for the leader. Employees on campus are no less influenced, and no less appreciative. Plus, a leader who wishes to transform the institution into an organization of social consequence cannot gain a sense of what its vision must be through filtered lenses. He or she must feel, smell, taste, and experience the needs and desires of those the college serves.

HEARING THE REAL MESSAGE

The second complication with effective listening is that even when the leader is seen in an informal, walking-around situation, coworkers are inclined to view the occasional visit as artificial, intrusive, and evaluative. I am reminded of a research approach used in the behavioral sciences to which I was exposed as a graduate student. Called Participant Observation, the method requires the researcher to become so completely immersed in the community being studied that those being observed engage in their normal activities without self-consciousness, without altering behavior as a result of being observed. One of the oft-sighted shortcomings of Participant Observation is that it is difficult to become fully assimilated into the new culture, and even more difficult to know when that has happened. There is still debate, for example, about whether the noted anthropologist Margaret Mead reported accurately on the mating habits of the Islanders about whom she wrote in *Coming of Age in Samoa* or was simply toyed with by the young women she observed.

Most of us know our general institutional cultures well, but not necessarily the cultures of the college's subgroups or of key community constituencies. What is important to that group of maintenance workers? To other hourly staff? To the Vietnamese refugee community? What are the major faculty concerns of the moment? Do the math and physical sciences faculty have the same vision for the institution held by faculty in business or the humanities? Not much candid communication flows during these walk about drop-in moments, and they provide practically no opportunity to learn about what others dream for themselves. Even when conversation seems free and casual, colleagues who view themselves as subordinate are carefully guarding what they say and measuring its effect. This is not to suggest that "walking around" involvement in the institution is not important to keep in touch, but few of us do it well, no matter how well intentioned. And even when done with regularity, it must be accompanied by a keen ability to listen and accept.

LEARNING TO LISTEN

For many, listening has become a lost art. We hear, but often fail to *listen*. Robert Greenleaf noted: "Persons who achieve *high* leadership positions are generally not good listeners. They are too assertive. They have to *learn* to listen."[4] Listening is an act of submission, of respect and interest; an active intellectual exercise which requires focused attention on what is being said with a desire to understand. The prayer of St. Francis was, "Lord, grant that I may not seek so much to be understood as to understand." To fail to listen effectively is to fail to convey genuine caring, and consequences can be disastrous for even the best intentioned leader.

A colleague whom I would classify as among the brightest and most able I have known in terms of abilities to understand and apply sound "textbook" management principles has repeatedly found herself in trouble as a leader. The diagnosis at each place has been, "She doesn't listen." As I visited with employees at colleges where she served, typical comments were:

> "Her mind is obviously somewhere else when I talk to her and she often interrupts."

> "She is preparing her answers before she hears the question."

> "It's apparent she doesn't really care what I think or have to say."

By contrast, there are those who have managed, through genuine displays of interest in faculty, students, and community members, to gain a trust that allows open dialogue and listening opportunities. Mel George, who presided over St. Olaf College before returning from retirement to head the University of Missouri system for a brief interim period, was such a leader. An associate of George's stated: "You can talk to Mel about anything—good or bad. If it's critical of something going on at the University, you know he will consider and act on it if it has merit."

A colleague learned a great deal about Mel George as a leader when he visited St. Olaf College in Minnesota while George was serving as its president. On one of the bulletin boards was an announcement of a senior music recital with a note that the student would be accompanied by Mel George. Curious about the existence of this second Mel George, pianist, the colleague attended the recital, and there was President George at the piano. He was acknowledged as the accompanist without fanfare. Though this act of service obviously fell within an area of special musical interest, it demonstrates a willingness by the president to be directly involved in the lives and activities of members of the campus community, quite a contrast to James Fisher's "intentioned separation." The implication is that listening requires presence, empathy, genuine interest, and a common sense of meaning.

Greenleaf suggested that the first impulse of the servant leader must be to listen, not to talk, and recommended regular periods of time dedicated to improving listening skills. He advised:

> Everyone who aspires to *strength* should consciously practice listening, regularly. Every week, set aside an hour to listen to somebody who might have something to say that will be of interest. It should be conscious practice in which all of the impulses to argue, inform, judge and "straighten out" the other person are denied. Every response should be calculated to reflect interest, understanding, seeking for more knowledge. Practice listening for brief periods, too. Just thirty seconds of concentrated listening make the difference between understanding and not understanding something important.[5]

A valuable Confucian concept is what the Chinese sage referred to as "The Rectification of Names." To Confucius, meaning and understanding could only be assured if those speaking knew that the terms they used had common definition—that when you said "tenure" and I heard "tenure," we knew that we were talking about the same idea. You might say, for example, "I think faculty tenure has become a problem for us." I could easily understand you to mean that the "tenure system" has become problematic, when your intent was to convey that the loss of a number of our long-term faculty through retirement has changed our sense of institutional history and tradition. Unless I asked for clarification, I might begin to convey to others what I thought was your message and completely misrepresent your thoughts. To avoid this, one can easily make genuine questioning a part of listening habits with, "Elaborate on that for me," or, "Explain a bit more what you mean by that," being all that is needed to turn hearing into listening and understanding.

FORMALIZED LISTENING

Because of the size of many of our institutions and communities and the complexities of our days, most of us need more formal ways to listen to what is happening—to learn what those we serve want. Peter Senge quotes former chair of Motorola, Bob Galvin, as having said, "My job is to listen to what the organization is trying to say, and then make sure that it gets forcefully articulated."[6] Beyond the techniques of "walking around," there are a number of simple ways to structure listening.

Several years ago, the academic and student services deans at a nearby college decided that the institution made too many assumptions about what students wanted from their college experience and about how successfully student interests were being met. Part of the difficulty arose from the changing nature of the student body, which had become much less traditional, less residential, and more diverse. To address the situation, the application form was altered to ask students to state an educational objective—receive a degree, take a few classes for personal enrichment, improve job readiness skills, gain new skills to use in current employment.

A writing sample, taken during orientation and used as part of English placement, asked students to elaborate on the stated educational objective. Faculty advisors were provided with this information to help focus advising sessions on specific student desires.

Perhaps the most useful of the innovations in terms of hearing student voices was the initiation of what the college called its Crest experience. At the end of the final semester, a day was set aside for small focus groups, using faculty members as facilitators. With tests out of the way and grades behind them, students were invited to talk candidly in groups of 7 to 10 about their experience at the college, with particular attention given to how well the college had helped students meet their individual goals. A recorder unobtrusively made notes of the comments, and they were distributed back through the faculty and administration. According to the deans, students were remarkably candid about their experiences, good and bad, and the Crest day structured a way for the college to *listen* to one of the groups it was created to serve. For large universities, the Crest type activity may appear to be prohibitively cumbersome—but not if conducted on a departmental basis where much of the listening needs to occur.

In the opening chapter, I mentioned the use of evaluation as a means of giving voice to others within the organization. If an academic leader wants to know what people want from the college and what they think about its performance, he or she simply needs to ask. Invite everyone who is subordinate to anonymously evaluate the leader. If president, invite everyone. Ask how well the leader listens. Ask how concerned the institution is about helping individuals achieve personal goals. Ask where the academic soft spots are within the college or university. People will be glad to respond. Code the evaluations to separate response data by employee segment while still maintaining anonymity; faculty, hourly employees, professional staff. The responses will differ significantly by group and disaggregating the data will provide a clearer view of unique group interests. Then *listen* to what people say.

There will, of course, always be those who use the opportunity to air personal grievances or who try to indicate that single irritations are the norm, but that can also be useful if kept in perspective. More valuable is comparative information, data that indicates that attitudes are changing from year to year, or that one segment of the college community feels quite differently than another about a key element of vision or practice.

One president who annually asks all in the college community to evaluate his performance noted that responses by the hourly staff reflected a sense of isolation, of not feeling informed about activities and goals, and of not feeling "important" to what the college was trying to achieve. He spoke with the president of the group's association who pointed out that though the president met regularly with his cabinet and was often present at various faculty meetings, he never met with the hourly employees. "You may not think we matter that much," the representative added, "but you'd be surprised at how often we are the first people prospective students talk to when they come here ... and how often they ask us what's going on."

The president made two simple changes, and the next year's evaluations showed dramatic improvement in areas related to communication and involvement. He began attending a portion of the association's meetings and giving a college update, sharing at each opportunity something about the vision he had for the college. He also modified a portion of the presemester faculty workshop day to include all personnel, with some jointly conducted sessions and some designed specifically for hourly employees. The change was simply one of hearing and valuing every voice.

While serving in a presidency, I requested evaluations of my performance by everyone in the college community for nearly 20 years. It was the most painful part of the annual review, because each year I wanted to see that we had miraculously become problem free, and that everyone felt uniformly positive about our direction. Plus, I wanted to be loved. It never happened. I invariably got zinged by several people, and an even greater number pointed out areas that needed improvement. I learned, though, that even in the zingers, there was a kernel of truth that demanded attention. When themes recurred, I was reminded that even though I may have taken steps to address a concern a year before, I either took the wrong action or did not follow through well ... or possibly, I did not really listen the first time.

Greenleaf observed, "The best test of whether we are communicating ... is to ask ourselves first: Are we really listening?"[7] Good listening is the initial step to good leadership. For the service-directed leadership our future demands, without listening, there will be no understanding, and without understanding, no direction for service.

NOTES

1. 10:37 Luke KJV.
2. An allusion to the captain of the Enterprise on the *Star Trek* television series.
3. Kina Mallard, "Management by Walking Around and the Department Chair," *The Department Chair* 10 (1999), quoting W. Edwards Deming, http://secure.aidcvt.com/ank/ProdDetails.asp?ID=DCHAIRSUB (accessed June 13, 2006).
4. Robert K. Greenleaf, *On Being a Servant Leader,* ed. Don M. Frick and Larry C. Spears (San Francisco: Jossey-Bass, 1990), 303.
5. Ibid., 70.
6. Peter M. Senge, "Robert Greenleaf's Legacy: A New Foundation for Twenty-First Century Institutions," in *Reflections on Leadership,* ed. Larry C. Spears (New York: John Wiley & Sons, 1995), 229.
7. Robert K. Greenleaf, *The Servant as Leader* (Indianapolis, IN: Robert K. Greenleaf Center, 1991), 10.

CHAPTER

Renewing the Social Contract

Human history becomes more and more a race between education and catastrophe.

—H. G. Wells

There was a time, beyond most of our memories, when undergraduate education was the primary raison d'être for all colleges and universities. That has since changed, at least in much of the four-year sector, resulting in a downward spiral in both the emphasis placed on the undergraduate curriculum and the quality of its offerings. Admittedly, much of the basis for this assertion is anecdotal and suppositional—because higher education has religiously refused to assess undergraduate performance by any uniform standard. Yet, one need spend only an evening visiting with university faculty to learn that undergraduate students are often seen as a necessary inconvenience, and little more than the tuition fodder that feeds the research and graduate education beast that is the modern university.

Because of the central focus of their "teaching mission," community colleges have remained much more actively engaged in finding and applying effective tools for undergraduate instruction. But here, again, few can demonstrate what actually happens to students in terms of academic achievement while with the college. Students can just as easily complete an associate degree with an academically soft program of study as they can the first two years of a university education. At the average college, completion of a degree is simply no assurance that the graduate is a well-informed or particularly well-educated citizen.

Yet tuition for undergraduates continues to rise faster than the consumer price index, annually requiring a greater share of disposable family income. In many cases, new tuition revenue is not committed to improving undergraduate teaching and learning.[1] Freshman classes remain large and impersonal with limited rigor, while new revenue is committed to elaborate buildings, research agendas, and salaries to attract distinguished faculty who contribute little or nothing to the undergraduate experience.

The result has been a largely uninformed population, even among the college educated. High school graduation rates in the United States at the end of the twentieth century were 71percent, meaning that over a quarter of our young people were entering the marketplace with less than a high school diploma.[2] Of high school graduates, only approximately 57 percent went directly to college, reducing each ninth grade class of 1,000 to 400 immediate college enrollees.[3] Of these 400, roughly half attended two-year colleges and half four-year institutions. Of the four-year college attendees, a quarter did not return after the first year, and half did not graduate. So only 1 in 10 of our class of 1,000 ninth graders went directly from high school to a four-year college and completed a baccalaureate degree.[4]

Fortunately, our American system provides multiple points of access, and largely due to our innovative twentieth century creation, the community college, we now see approximately a quarter of our 25 to 34 year old population with a BA (bachelor of art) or above. Recent reports indicate, however, that many who graduate from our institutions of higher learning do not have the basic skills we would expect of a college educated person.[5]

These numbers should be an embarrassment to us as a nation, and of particular concern to public policymakers who are seeking ways to sustain a robust economy. The greatest challenge facing leadership in all of education in this century will be to refocus learning where students and the public at large need it to be—on precollegiate and undergraduate achievement. For community college leadership, the task is to insure that the 50 percent of undergraduates who enter their doors are either rigorously prepared for baccalaureate transfer, or have skill sets that provide adaptable employment opportunities. For universities, primary attention must return to the undergraduate curriculum, while still maintaining the productive part of the university research agenda. This simply cannot be done without redefining the roles of the community college and the university, at a time when the faculty is perhaps more powerful as a controlling agent in higher education than it has ever been.

Our social agreement with students and with our funding "stakeholders,"—whether we be two- or four-year colleges, public or private—is that, if students graduate from our institutions with a credential, they will have the skills, knowledge, and analytical abilities needed to play a productive role in modern society. If that is not the agreement, we need to let the public know, because they believe it to be. Yet we know that, for most colleges and universities, some who have not mastered content are passed out of classes, and with these cumulative passes, are granted degrees. And this is occurring at a time when we can least afford it as a nation.

Increasingly strong education systems in Asia are producing graduates who are drawing even traditional white-collar employment to China and India: finance, insurance, engineering, graphic design, and medicine. I noticed, for example, that the cover design work for *Declining by Degrees,* a collection of articles generally critical of the state of U.S. college education, was done in Chennai, India. The publisher chose not to rely on resident graduates of our own educational system for this design work, but illustrated the reality that work based upon brain capital no longer needs to be place-centered and can be done from anywhere. Much of it can be done less expensively abroad.

This ability to move work around the world is a central theme of Thomas Friedman's best seller, *The World Is Flat,* in which he quotes Jaithirth Rao, an Indian accountant, as stating that skilled accountants located in India can easily do most of the routine accounting being processed in the United States at a fraction of the cost. "The accountant who wants to stay in business in America will be the one who focuses on designing creative, complex strategies," Rao explains—not the run of the mill B or C student who skated by as an undergraduate. Rao observes that America's competitive strength has been that it is "always on the edge of the next creative wave."[6] But without a talented and competent pool of undergraduates, we will neither recognize these waves as they arrive, nor have the creative sense to climb aboard. With inexpensive labor already drawing most manufacturing to other countries, we can ill afford to lose our service and professional businesses. We are, as H. G. Wells predicted, shaping a history that is a race between education and economic catastrophe.

The role of the new leader in higher education must therefore become one of restoring the primacy and rigor of the undergraduate learning experience. The greatest commitment of service must be to our social, cultural, and economic future—to revitalizing and reenergizing undergraduate education—with service to students, the public, and to faculty shaped to achieve that end. We cannot abandon our commitment to significant research, but we can no longer afford to support "make-work" or inconsequential research, nor can we allow the research agenda to redirect our resources from those who will provide the intellectual and financial capital to maintain that research into the future. We must create, again, a large pool of undergraduates with broad-based, liberal educations that provide a grasp of issues that are shaping our time, the historical and intellectual context for those issues, and the analytical skills to formulate direction and solutions for the future. To provide this service, leaders must themselves understand and acknowledge the historical currents that carried us to this state of disconnection, and must craft strategies to redirect those currents.

THE STUDENT/FACULTY DISCONNECT

Arthur Levine notes that fewer than one in five of today's college students is what we once viewed as traditional: just out of high school, attending full-time, and living on campus. This new majority, he says:

want their colleges nearby and offering classes during the most convenient times for them, preferably twenty-four hours a day. They want easy accessible parking, no lines, and a helpful, polite, and efficient staff. They want accessible, high quality instruction by professors who are up to date in their fields, who return assignments quickly, who offer useful evaluation of student work, and who are expert at teaching. They want all of these things at low cost. In short, they are asking for convenience, service, quality, and low cost.[7]

Levine describes faculty, on the other hands, as wanting:

small numbers of advisees, light dissertation loads, and classes. They also want to be able to offer courses in their specialty areas, to offer classes at times that are convenient to them, and to avoid offering required and introductory courses outside their field. In addition, faculty would like to be able to take time off from classes to attend professional meetings and to have graduate students to assist them with their teaching and research. Time and support for research are essential, particularly at research universities and the most selective colleges.[8]

In his eloquent history of the development of higher education in the United States, Frederick Rudolph describes the evolution of the academy from its colonial beginnings to the time of the initial publication of Rudolph's history in 1962. Though he stresses that undergraduate education remained central to the mission of American colleges and universities through the first half of the twentieth century, he notes that, as the century began, the powerful influences of the German university's emphasis on scholarship were reshaping the role of the professor.[9]

Christopher Lucas describes the emerging "university" as being shaped by the thinking of prominent academic leaders in the second half of the nineteenth century who had either studied in Germany or had visited the great universities of Berlin, Heidelberg, and Leipzig, and were enthralled with the idea of disinterested scholarship and research.[10] The ideal professor became one who was free to study and learn, to teach whatever he saw as important to his discipline—but with the greater emphasis on scholarly inquiry. (I use "he" here advisedly, since the early American professorate was an exclusively male domain.)

Rudolph cites an interview in *The Atlantic Monthly* from 1909 in which writer Abraham Flexner asked a college dean who the best teacher in his institution was, then asked whether the gentleman was likely to be promoted. After identifying the faculty member, the dean answered no. When asked why, the administrator's response was that "he hasn't done anything," meaning that he had not been actively involved in scholarly research and publication.[11] This same discussion could have occurred in any number of universities a century later, with teaching excellence remaining almost incidental to tenure and promotion, giving some credence to the quip attributed to John Ciardi that "a university is what a college becomes when the faculty loses interest in students."[12]

Murray Sperber attributes the roots of the final disconnect between undergraduate teaching and faculty priorities to the beginning of the space race in the mid- to late 1950s. Frightened by the prospects of a Cold War gap in military technology between the United States and the Soviet Union, the federal government flooded universities with research money, encouraging a proliferation of graduate programs and elevating the status of research and publication. Though the primary interest of the government was in science and technology, the explosion in graduate education was indiscriminate and crossed virtually every discipline. The result was a glut of PhD programs and of doctoral graduates in the social sciences, communications, and the fine arts who, to justify their existence, needed more graduate students in these disciplines, with continued emphasis on research and publication.[13] Scholarly journals and presses multiplied to provide outlets for the endless stream of "publish or perish" research, demanding greater specialization and esoterica in order to carve out areas of academic uniqueness.

I recall, as an undergraduate, sitting through a series of lectures by a professor who was researching the symbolic significance of the double-blossomed cherry tree in George Meredith's *The Egoist*. Later, as a professor, I used the double-blossomed cherry tree example to illustrate the degree to which research in many areas has reached the point of meaningless triviality. One graduate student observed that the study had undoubtedly honed the researcher's skills, better prepared him for future study, and made him better able to train other researchers in his area of English literature.

"To what end, though?" I asked. "His research wasn't read by more than a dozen people. He taught only a few undergraduate courses, and did not do that particularly well. What contribution was he making to the university's social contract with its constituents?"

"Research," she said, "has value in and of itself."

That seems to have become the mantra of university faculty. But at what cost?

As state and federal commitment to public education declined precipitously after the 1970s, universities faced two choices. They could eliminate costly graduate programs that were producing this voluminous and sometimes inconsequential research to once again focus on undergraduate education, or they could maintain the emphasis on graduate scholarship and replace lagging state and federal support with higher student fees, larger undergraduate classes, and less expensive ways of teaching lower division sections. But the reward system based on scholarship had become too entrenched—the appeal of being part of a so-called community of scholars too seductive. Student pools, bloated by the coming of age of the baby boomers, had provided all the students colleges and universities could manage during the 1960s and 70s, without requiring much in the way of customer service or incentives. The policies of these decades had also become codified to the degree that they were viewed as biblical in import, and bordering on heresy to challenge.

Much more recently, during a time of competitive enrollment and challenging financial times for a university, an associate graduate dean reflected the same archaic view of policy as supreme. When approached by faculty about numerous complaints from graduate applicants concerning failings in the admissions process—misplaced transcripts and graduate records exam scores, rude treatment when inquiring about the status of their applications—the dean's response was a throwback to the days of "If you build it, they will come:"

> I really find that hard to believe if these were students who followed directions and were "on the ball." If they weren't, then we probably don't want them in a doctoral program anyway.... I think we do better with students who realize that the opportunity to do doctoral work is a special one and who are appreciative of this opportunity. People do not have a right to a doctoral degree just because they want one or somebody tells them they should have one. If they really appreciate the opportunity, then they are going to take it on themselves to be sure all of their materials are submitted in a timely manner. They will read directions and attend to the smallest detail.... I'm sorry but I guess I'm losing my patience with people who put the procrastination of applicants back on the Graduate Education office and the Graduate School. The process has been the same for quite some time now and we've collectively explained it to so many faculty so often that there really isn't a reason that our faculty shouldn't know the process by now.

No consideration was given here to whether the complaints were legitimate, or to why, after all these explanations, even the faculty hadn't figured out the process. Students were seen as existing for the university, rather than the university for the students.

Undergraduate education as a priority was further eroded by the implementation of the Carnegie classification system of 1970, creating a hierarchy that moved beyond designating "type," but served to codify "status." By placing the Research I universities at the top, and moving down through Research II to the also-rans, faculty were also awarded status, with some of the finest teaching institutions included among the also-rans. Though recently redefined, the classifications are still ordered primarily by research involvement, with the lists topped by those with "very high research activity" and moving downward.[14]

The more recent phenomenon of media rating systems has done little to realign these priorities. Unable to credibly determine the quality of student learning, the ranking systems yielded to more easily quantifiable measures such as ratios of applications to admissions and quantifiable indicators of faculty scholarship. Through these collective developments, teaching and learning gradually became a casualty of the national research agenda of the Cold War.

THE SOCIAL DILEMMA

As a result, leaders in education now find themselves wrestling with three sets of expectations—two somewhat in harmony, and one in apparent conflict. Society wants universal access to an undergraduate system of higher education that produces academically astute, socially responsible, and economically productive citizens. Students want an affordable, convenient, applicable, and rigorous college education. Faculty, particularly in universities, want minimal course loads, arranged at times convenient to them, with maximum opportunity to work on their scholarly interests. Educational leadership does not stand at the junction of these interests, because they do not intersect. Instead, leaders stand between diverging lines of interest, and must determine how to bring them back together. The critical leadership questions become one of who must change direction to intersect, and how that change can be managed to "serve all concerned?"

Three compelling factors indicate that students and the public must determine the agenda for higher education, and faculty interests must be redirected. The first, and most urgent, is that these stated student and public interests are in line with what our best minds tells us we must do to survive as a viable social, economic, and cultural entity—develop a broad based, liberally and critically educated population. We know that our current commitment of faculty resources is not producing that outcome, so they must be redirected.

Secondly, the students and public—whether taxpayers, tuition payers, or donors—are supporting the enterprise. They are increasingly saying "We are not sure what we are getting for our investment. We want to have clearer indicators of the quality and appropriateness of the educational product and are not going to pay more until we see the evidence." Faculty see the declines in state and federal support, see the shift in tuition-paying students to more economical and teaching-centered community colleges and to results producing for-profit institutions, but have refused to embrace accountability-driven approaches to funding and quantitative measures of student learning. The public demand for accountability will not change. If we are to improve undergraduate education, faculty willingness to be accountable must change.

The third factor is closely related. The market will drive change. In a 2004 Survey of Public Opinion on Higher Education conducted by the *Chronicle of Higher Education,* the highest rated responsibility for colleges and universities was to "prepare its undergraduate students for a career." Seventy percent of respondents rated this obligation as "very important," and another 22 percent as "important." It was followed closely by "preparing students to be responsible citizens," with 67 percent and 18 percent respectively, and "prepare future leaders of society," with 66 percent and 21 percent. Also rated at the top with combined "very important" and "important" percentages in the upper 80s were "provide education to adults so they qualify for better jobs" and "offer a broad-based general education to undergraduate students." Although still seen as an important function, "discover more about the world through research" ranked 10th.

As an introduction to a speech on the importance of helping our students gain a global perspective, I asked a large, college-educated audience to identify the issues that most concerned them, as they looked at what their children would face in the next 25-year period. I anticipated that global conflict, environmental and ecological change, or the threat of endemic disease—all hotly debated topics in the news at the time—might top the list. But the number one concern by a significant margin was job security.

"I am not confident that my daughter will be able to compete in the global marketplace," one woman explained. "I fear that America is moving toward a second tier economic position in the world."

Perhaps these public priorities explain why in the same *Chronicle* survey, the level of public confidence in public community colleges was as high as for public four-year colleges and universities. The public wants education for employment. While private four-year colleges and universities led the list of educational institutions, with 48 percent of the public expressing "a great deal" of confidence and 43 percent expressing "some," the corresponding numbers for community colleges were 41 percent and 49 percent, respectively, and for four-year public colleges, 40 percent and 50 percent.[15]

These figures may open a window into understanding why enrollments have been shifting so dramatically over the past century. Community colleges, which celebrated their 100th year with the beginning of the new century, now enroll half of all undergraduates in public education, reflecting the public's interest in relevant education, delivered when and where consumers want it. They continue to grow at a faster rate than do public four-year colleges and universities, but neither sector is coming close to keeping pace with the private sector.

Between 1997 and 2002, four-year public college and university growth barely exceeded 1 percent per year, with community colleges growing at approximately twice that rate. The most remarkable growth was in the for-profit sector which sustained increases of over 13 percent annually during that period.[16] Some of my colleagues who say, partly tongue-in-cheek, that as long as public universities have Division 1 athletics they will be attractive to students, need to think again. The *Chronicle* survey mentioned above found that only 14 percent of those responding found "athletics for entertainment of the community" to be a "very important" role for colleges, with 19 percent seeing athletics as "important." This combined 33 percent was the lowest of the nineteen items on this portion of the survey, and fell below "encouraging students to study in other countries," (57%) and "provide cultural events for the community" (56%).[17]

We have, in this divergence in view and priority, the classic Follett creative conflict, although in this case, the conflict exists within and among players in the greater system of college education, rather than simply within the institutions themselves. Follett preferred to use the term "difference," and said of conflict that, "At the outset I should like to ask you to agree for the moment to think of conflict as neither good nor bad; to consider it without ethical pre-judgment; to think of it not as warfare, but as the appearance of difference, difference of opinions, of interests. For that is what conflict means—difference."[18] The difference in this case is that students and the public want undergraduate learning to be of primary importance for colleges and universities, while many universities have made it a third or fourth priority for faculty; after research, publication, and the related imperative of grant-writing. How does the leader, then, begin to address this critical difference?

The first step is to refuse to see it as insurmountable—as an irreconcilable difference. Follett advises:

As conflict—difference—is here in the world, as we cannot avoid it, we should, I think, use it. Instead of condemning it, we should set it to work for us. Why not? What does the mechanical engineer do with friction? Of course his chief job is to eliminate friction, but it is true that he also capitalizes friction. The transmission of power by belts depends on friction between the belt and the pulley. The friction between the driving wheel of the locomotive and the track is necessary to haul the train. All polishing is done by friction. The music of the violin we get by friction. We left the savage state when we discovered fire by friction. We talk of the friction of mind on mind as a good thing. So in business, too, we have to know when to try to eliminate friction and when to try to capitalize it, when to see what work we can make it do. That is what I wish to consider here, whether we can set conflict to work and make it *do* something for us.[19]

To determine how to make that friction work to our mutual advantage—to serve the interests of all concerned, we return again to another of the central Follett principles, the Law of the Situation. This principle asserts that, within the situation, if fully examined, lies the solution. It assumes that to reach an integrated solution, one that serves all by recognizing and embracing their needs, *all* of the elements of the conflict—of the differences—must be laid on the table for *all* to examine. No more secrets. So what are the components of this pervasive difference that is gradually degrading undergraduate higher education in the United States? Simply stated, they are that:

- students want an undergraduate education that prepares them to be economically competitive and socially and culturally aware;
- the general public wants a college educated population that can sustain the country's competitive position in the world, and maintain a civil and just society;
- colleges and universities want recognition and prestige, and the resources necessary to sustain whatever activity creates that status;
- faculty want personal recognition, security, and a sense of scholarly satisfaction from their work;
- the rewards system that has developed that both grants recognition and prestige to universities, and security and scholarly satisfaction to faculty is based on evaluative factors that do not further the primary interests of either students or the public at large.

It is especially noteworthy that there is nothing intrinsically incompatible about these desires. In fact, in the community college sector in higher education, they do not seem to be incompatible at all. Freshman and sophomore teaching and learning continue to be areas of primary focus, and a community college's reputation depends on how well it can demonstrate that it is achieving these student and public goals. Faculty at these institutions show greater job satisfaction than is typically exhibited by their four-year colleagues,[20] indicting that one can have a satisfying and productive academic career without the publications and research accompaniment.

The incompatibility at the university level arises because student learning and public service have been preempted by the research agenda. But the set of priorities listed above could be reconciled if universities, and those who rate and rank them, recognized high quality undergraduate education as being among the ways in which recognition, prestige, and resources could be gained. Faculty would in turn view excellence in teaching as an acceptable avenue to recognition, security, and personal reward. As leadership theorists Alan Kolp and Peter Rea note, "Difficulty arises … when we want one goal and reward another."[21]

According to Follett, the conflict exists because primary goals of participants have become incompatible. But in this case, they are not irreconcilable. The able leader in education must be able to assess all of these desires and place them in balance—neither subordinating the wishes of students or the general public to the prestige interests of the institution or the scholarly goals of faculty, nor minimizing the importance of the latter. The leader must find ways to present each of these constituent priorities openly and publicly, with an infectious conviction that, if all can view the situation in its entirety and have free and candid input into its resolution, an integrated solution lies within it.

To do so, however, presidents must have the power to insist that all parties have equal voice at the table and that the desires of each stakeholder be given equal import. This requires the right, power, and ability to intervene with some protection when interest groups attempt to impose their own wills at the expense of others. Given the current state of higher education, there must be a redistribution of power to put college and university presidents back into a position where they can insist that students and the public be heard and that their needs and interests are acknowledged and met. In many institutions, that power has been either lost or seriously diminished, and must be restored if the academy, particularly in the public sector, is to continue to be socially and economically relevant.

NOTES

1. Arthur Levine, "Worlds Apart: Disconnects Between Students and Their Colleges," *Declining by Degrees*, ed. Richard H. Hersh and John Merrow (New York: Palgrave Macmillan, 2005), 156.

2. Jay P. Greene, "High School Graduation Rates in the United States," *Civic Report*, Manhattan Institute for Policy Research, April 2002, http://www.manhattan-institute.org/html/cr_baeo.htm.

3. The National Center for Higher Education Management Systems, "College Going Rates of High School Graduates—Directly from H.S," *The NCHEMS Information Center for State Higher Education Policymaking and Analysis* 2002, http://www.higheredinfo.org/dbrowser/index.php?submeasure=63&year=2002&level=nation&mode=data&state=0.

4. "College Graduation Rates Steady Despite Increase In Enrollment," *ACT Newsroom*, 15 November 2002, http://www.act.org/news/releases/2002/11–15–02.html.

5. *Declining by Degrees*, DVD, produced by Learning Matters, Inc. (Public Broadcasting Service, 2005).

6. Thomas Friedman, *The World Is Flat: A Brief History of the Twenty-first Century* (New York: Farrar, Straus and Giroux, 2005), 11–15.

7. Levine, 158.

8. Ibid., 164.

9. Frederick Rudolph, *The American College and University: A History* (Athens: University of Georgia Press, 1990), 445, 494.

10. Christopher J. Lucas, *American Higher Education: A History* (New York: St. Martin's Press, 1994), 171.

11. Rudolph, 402.

12. This quote is often attributed to John Ciardi, but its origin seems uncertain.

13. Murray Sperber, "How Undergraduate Education Became College Lite—and a Personal Apology," in *Declining by Degrees*, ed. Richard H. Hersh and John Merrow (New York: Palgrave Macmillan, 2005), 132–133.

14. Audrey Williams June, "College Classifications Get an Overhaul," *Chronicle of Higher Education*, 3 March 2006, A25.

15. "Chronicle Survey of Public Opinion on Higher Education, *Chronicle of High Education*, 7 May 2004, A12–13.

16. National Center for Educational Statistics, "Enrollment in Title IV institutions, by degree-granting status, level and control of institution, attendance status, gender, and race/ethnicity: United States, fall 2002," http://nces.ed.gov/das/library/tables_listings/show_nedrc.asp?rt=p&tableID=1570; National Center for Educational Statistics, "Total enrollment in Title IV eligible postsecondary institutions, by degree-granting status, control, and level of institution: 50 states and the District of Columbia, fall 1997," http://nces.ed.gov/quicktables/Detail.asp?Key=318.

17. "Chronicle Survey," A13.

18. Mary Parker Follett, *Dynamic Administration: The Collected Papers of Mary Parker Follett*, ed. Elliot M. Fox and L. Urwick (London: Pitman, 1973), 30.

19. Ibid., 30–31.

20. Arthur M. Cohen and Florence Brawer, *The American Community College*, 4th ed. (San Francisco: Jossey-Bass, 2003), 93.

21. Alan Kolp and Peter Rea, *Leading with Integrity: Character-Based Leadership* (Cincinnati, OH: Atomic Dog Publishing, 2006), 80.

CHAPTER 8

Empowering Toward Service

> Servant Leadership deals with the reality of power in everyday life—its legitimacy, the ethical restraints upon it and the beneficial results that can be attained through the appropriate use of power.
>
> —*New York Times*

A recent call from a headhunter seeking information about a colleague who practices Servant-Leadership illustrated the delicate balancing act facing the president who recognizes the necessity of seeing leadership as an act of service.

"If you asked both this person's greatest admirers and detractors what they liked or disliked about this leader," she asked, "what would they say?"

My immediate thought was that these two groups would probably base their responses on the same characteristic. Admirers would praise the leader for being so inclusive, for involving as many people as possible in the institution in organizational governance. Detractors would criticize the individual based on what they would label indecisiveness, stating that they wished she would just make decisions quickly and do her job, leaving them to do theirs.

This is only one of a series of paradoxes that present themselves daily to the highly involving leader and raise critical questions about the exercise of power within an organization. How does one take into the account the interests, wishes, and needs of all stakeholders and still get decisions made? How can a leader further his or her own visionary interests while satisfying the needs and desires of others? If service to others is the aim, how does the leader resolve conflicts when he or she views a recommendation as being out of sync with the best interests of the institution? And what happens when the leader disagrees with what appear to be consensus views by others on an issue for which the leader will be held responsible? These questions require that we examine what power means, how it is distributed and exercised within the servant-led organization, and how it relates to "trust" and "consensus," two leader-as-servant essentials.

THE NATURE OF POWER

There are any number of lists of the kinds of power that exists or can exist within an organization. The first formal introduction to organizational management that I remember with any clarity was Hersey and Blanchard's *Management of Organizational Behavior,* a reference to which I still return on occasion because of its succinct analysis of organizational types, leadership models, and individual motivation. Drawing upon the work of Amitai Etzioni, Hersey and Blanchard define power as "the ability to induce or influence behavior," and divide it into two categories: position power and personal power.[1] Kolp and Rea are among many who elaborate on these divisions by delineating ways in which both positional and personal power can be exercised, as power derived from the ability to reward, coerce, manage information, demonstrate expertise, or influence through referential deference or prestige.[2]

Many current management texts are inclined to define power in even more controlling terms, as Moorhead and Griffin do in *Organizational Behavior: Managing People and Organizations.* For them, power is "the potential ability of a person or group to exercise control over another person or group. Power is distinguished from influence by its reliance on control."[3]

It is little wonder that the transition in American management from top-down organizations to more horizontal, participatory models has been difficult when many managers have been weaned on definitions of power that focus so specifically on "control over." These definitions ignore, or at least minimize, the value of cooperative power, the power Mary Parker Follett describes as power-with. Power-with assumes that effective power can grow from a collaborative examination of a situation—directed, but not forced by the leader—and can result in a mutually agreed upon course of action that is integrative in nature and recognized as meeting some of the interests of all involved.

Greenleaf delineates three traditional types of power: coercive, manipulative, and persuasive. For Greenleaf, the first two are exercises of power-over, with coercive being the power of threat—"Do this or else." Manipulative power guides and influences the follower by taking advantage of incomplete understanding or deception—"Trust me on this." Persuasive power for Greenleaf is power-with and helps the follower arrive at a sense of rightness about a decision by creating understanding leading to intuitive commitment: "Do you see how we can all benefit from this?"[4] Greenleaf goes on to argue that persuasive power is most effective when it is the power of consensus, with consensus being a method of utilizing persuasive power in groups.

Covey, in *Principle-Centered Leadership*, defines power as coercive, utilitarian, or principle-centered. He describes coercive power much as Greenleaf does, but sees utility power as that which provides the follower with some desired benefit—the power of useful exchange. Principle-centered power, according to Covey, is power based on trust that the leader is sincerely trying to accomplish mutually desirable goals and is doing it in an admirable and honorable way. Covey states: "Principle-centered power occurs when the cause or purpose or goal is believed in as deeply by the followers as by the leaders."[5] Both Greenleaf's "persuasive power" and Covey's "principle-centered power" exemplify power-with as it should be exercised by the leader as servant.

EXERCISING POWER-WITH

As a quick review, Mary Follett maintained that organizational life involved the constant resolution of conflicts or differences—mostly minor, some major—which result from one of two conditions: disagreement about institutional goals and direction, or lack of understanding about how the goals and direction can help members of the organization fulfill personal desires. Organizational effectiveness results from laying all of those personal interests and desires on the table, evaluating how they mesh with institutional goals, and working toward integrating the two. There is an assumption in this approach that each individual initially comes to the organization believing that it can assist with achieving at least *some* of the individual's desires. The process of integration becomes one of identifying what those are and working to establish the best fit between individual desires and organizational purposes.

On occasion, when honest effort is made to examine personal desires, some employees discover that there are *not* those areas where integration with institutional goals can occur, and the employer and employee find it in their best interest to look elsewhere for a better match. Among the dozens of resignations and the occasional dismissals that I have seen result from this realization, I can think of only one case in which the employee did not find a better "fit" after leaving the college. In that one situation, a dismissal was based upon the employee's constant need to exercise power-over, and unwillingness to work in a power-with organization. In the person's career since, that inability has continued to be a problem, and the individual has found it difficult to work effectively in any organizational setting.

Follett maintained that to find the *best* solutions, all concerned must objectively and dispassionately look for them. Once the solution is recognized, each person then exercises the power of his or her function to enact that solution—combining individual power with that of the others involved. The obvious value of broad review of the problem, and involvement in the solution, is the sense of ownership each then takes in the result. But there is another equally positive value to the process.

THE VALUE OF DIVERSITY

I worked for many years with a person who had a particular knack for seeing solutions in a problem that no one else recognized. He had an uncanny ability, as the cliché encourages, to think outside of the box. He is a person with a basic entrepreneurial flair, a man who is always searching for an idea that will help him create a product to seal his fortune. The same thinking always surfaced when we were struggling with a problem at the college. In many cases, he did not say much when the discussion began, but the wheels were almost audibly whirring. Often a suggestion made by another member of the group became the mutually agreed upon solution, but on occasion, he would say: "You know, there may be a completely different way to look at this issue." He would then present a solution that, though occasionally involving a somewhat greater degree of risk, obviously produced a better result if successful.

Due partly to his input and partly to other lessons of experience, I have come to appreciate the great differences in the ways people think and process information—the basis for much of modern learning theory. Some thinkers are highly sequential, able to order facts in a logical and systematic way. If an important piece of data is missing, they recognize it.

Others are holistic thinkers, occasionally finding the "Sequentials" frustratingly caught up in detail. The holistic, global thinkers have a way of cutting through piles of detail and quickly seeing an array of possible solutions. Sequentials can find these holistic thinkers infuriatingly irrational, particularly when the solutions seem logical, but the logic isn't evident. "Where in the world did that idea come from?," the Sequentials will say, still engaged in sorting and prioritizing information. Left to work on problems alone, Sequentials can drown in the details and the Holistics can completely overlook a critical ingredient. Put together, and allowed to attack problems with their own unique intellectual gifts, the results can be astounding. Power-over negates much of this value. Power-with cultivates it.

I have also become appreciatively aware of the special skills women bring to decision making. Emphasis on equality of opportunity, as critically important as it is, cannot deny the fact that there is not complete similarity between the sexes. Speaking in a very general way, women bring certain skills to discussion and problem solving that men often lack—or at least display less willingly. Sally Helgesen, in *The Female Advantage*, does a masterful job of describing what I have observed in practice—that women possess an integrating and relating ability that many men either do not possess, or choose not to exercise as freely and openly.[6] Anyone who has spent much time in problem solving sessions is familiar with the situation where, as the discussion progresses, one of the women involved will begin to solicit thoughts from nonparticipants, correlate ideas that have come up at different points in the deliberation, and draw important relationships. Perhaps women are responding to having been historically ignored and, as a result, become much more conscious of the need for inclusiveness.

Cultural diversity introduces many of the same benefits to problem solving, particularly now that organizations are so culturally diverse. Living abroad for a number of years, both in Europe and in the Middle East, taught me that various cultures have uniquely useful world views and uniquely effective ways to resolve conflict. This becomes particularly important as our institutions become more diverse and more heavily engaged in global education.

POWER AS A COLLECTIVE ENDEAVOR

Warren Bennis notes that "no matter how wise, shrewd, or visionary a leader is, a corporation is a collective endeavor, and it needs the collective wisdom of all of its employees to function at the optimum level."[7] This simply cannot happen without also viewing power as a collective activity. The principle of power-with is so central to syncretic leadership that a service-centered leader cannot be fully successful without it. Yet, the old adage that power corrupts is no less true today than it has ever been, and even the best intentioned leaders are easily seduced by finding suddenly that they can not only get what they want through the exercise of power, but that others are more than anxious to please them. Greenleaf called power the "virus" that has killed the spirit to serve in leadership. He observed:

> It seems an unrealistic pipe dream even to think about organized human activity without giving power to some people to push other people around. Heavy-handed or benign, I suspect that both holding and using power as it is commonly accepted are destructive of human spirit in both the powerholder and the subject. If we are to move toward a more servant-led society, it is imperative that we find a better way to assign power (if we have to assign it at all) than we have traditionally done and are doing. Otherwise, these institutions of ours will continue to grind down human spirit on a mammoth scale. We will not have many servants, and we will have a weaker society.[8]

Power will always be misused, but its misuse can be moderated by spreading it out across the organization. It is as dangerous when held exclusively by an employee association as by a president and, as Follett suggested, the organization must be designed in such a way that power follows function. No function should hold power to such a degree that its abuse can go unchecked and can be destructive to the whole. On the positive side, it must also be distributed in such a way that power can easily be combined to reach critical decisions easily and quickly, with the best input of all concerned stakeholders.

I recently observed a simple but convincing example of the effectiveness of power as a collective endeavor. A committee at a small college had been charged with addressing student concerns, uncovered through an exit survey administered to each graduate. The group was responding to a recurring complaint about incidental course fees. Students were not objecting to paying them, but complained that they were becoming so numerous and haphazard that students were unable to anticipate costs accurately and were not being given satisfying reasons for dramatic differences that appeared to be for the same service. Technology fees for computer use in the Business Department, for example, were substantially different than were computer use fees in the English Department.

During the process of several weeks that resolved the issue, useful input came not only from the Business office, where the fee was administered, but from one of the admissions staff, a member of the English faculty who served on the committee, a records clerk in the Registrar's office, and a financial aid counselor. Each contribution significantly affected the final decision, which turned out to be remarkably successful.

Yet bringing about change is rarely that simple. Earlier chapters have illustrated that the needs and interests of undergraduate students and the general public have been subordinated, in many cases, to the interests of those who support light faculty teaching responsibility, an emphasis on research and publication, and course schedules driven by faculty interest. Clearly, there is not a balance of power within much of higher education, and the influences of the faculty research agenda and of media-driven "best institution" rating systems have overwhelmed our underrepresented voices. After reestablishing undergraduate teaching and learning as a first priority in higher education, a second critical responsibility of the twenty-first century leader must be to reestablish a balance of power that enables this realignment to occur.

RE-EMPOWERING THE PRESIDENCY

Two factors stand as what often seem immovable barriers to organizational change in the academy: an imbalance of power in favor of the faculty, and entrenched organizational processes that impede service-centered decision making. More will be said about processes as impediments in the next chapter.

To say that faculty exercise too much power within higher education misrepresents the condition. Significant power is not "too much" if it is appropriate to role and responsibility. Admittedly, the faculty role is major, and they have monumental responsibility. The imbalances that occur are not reflections of inordinate amounts of power, but of insufficient power from other stakeholders to insure balance. Power is the ability to enact change, or to prevent change from being enacted, and when one party in a multiparty partnership is able to do either at will, power is not in balance.

Few boards and presidents have faithfully and forcefully represented student and public interests when establishing policy. When push comes to shove in redefining mission, role, and scope, boards and administrations have too often allowed faculty power—generally a reflection of perceived self-interest—to overwhelm the poorly represented power of these other groups. Boards and presidents who have the best interests of *all* stakeholders at heart—who are committed to strengthening the institution as a whole to insure long-term growth and solvency—must be in a position to balance the needs of these stakeholders against faculty self-interest. Shortly after Charles Eliot assumed the presidency at Harvard in 1869 and began the process of shaping it as a national model of higher learning, one of the medical faculty commented, "How is it that this faculty has gone for eighty years managing its own affairs and doing it well—and now within three or four months it is proposed to change all our modes of carrying on the school?" Eliot's reply was, "I can answer [the] question very easily. There is a new president."[9]

This may seem on its surface to fly in the face of power-with, but it is, in fact, essential for power-with to exist. Power-with assumes the inability of one interest group to block other stakeholders from pursuing mutual interests. Additionally, the final "approval" for critical decisions about the future of the institution cannot be left to a person or group that does not have to bear full and immediate responsibility and accountability for the decision.

Faculty are rarely in a position, individually or collectively, to see or know what will serve all institutional stakeholders most successfully. They are an interest group, and well-positioned to represent their own interests. They must have primary voice in determining curricular matters—but not absolute voice. The cloistering effect of the academy discussed in earlier chapters creates blinders, or at least shelters many faculty from the harsh realities and monumental changes occurring in much of public life. Presidents often have been equally cloistered, but it is part of their role to get in touch with that reality and insure that the institution responds to it and to the needs of other interest groups who must exercise their power through the presidency.

The responsibility to grant and protect this power lies with institutional governing boards, and this chapter is as much for them as it is for administrative leaders. Boards must grant and protect the authority and power to presidents to accomplish four ends:

1. To reestablish the primacy of undergraduate teaching and learning.
2. To forge an undergraduate curriculum that adequately prepares students for the global realities of the twenty-first century.
3. To represent the interests of students and the general public from a power position equal to any other within the institution.
4. To be the final voice in critical decisions affecting the future of the institution.

Point one, above, has already been explained in some detail. The second point is discussed in the next chapter, and point three in Chapter 11. We will close here by elaborating on the importance of point four.

Boards hire chief administrators to administer, then often fail them in one of two destructive ways. They either allow other entities within the organization *who cannot be held accountable* to thwart or trump the decisions of the president, or the board does this itself. In either of these cases, the board is holding a person responsible for decisions he or she is not being granted the power to make, while not holding accountable those who are exercising greatest influence over the decisions. Either of these actions is ethically and administratively irresponsible.

John Carver's Policy Governance model provides a sensible and defensible process for establishing an appropriate relationship between a board and college president, as well as for allocating roles and responsibilities. The model essentially dictates that the board's responsibility is to define the policy parameters within which the president must operate—the legal, ethical, and performance expectations of the position. As long as the president operates within those limits and achieves the performance objectives agreed upon, the board has a responsibility to stay out of the way—to keep its nose out of administrative matters. If the CEO acts illegally, unethically, or does not achieve agreed upon performance expectations, he or she can then be evaluated accordingly, and can lose the position. But to evaluate that performance honestly, the president must be empowered to be the final decision maker.[10]

If the board and president have agreed as institutional objectives to reestablish the primacy of the undergraduate curriculum and, in doing so, the president runs afoul of the faculty, the board must stand behind the president as long as the action is reasonable, ethical, and consistent with the agreed upon objective. In states where some institutional boards are elected and where special interest groups manage to get board members elected who represent their interests, these members have a responsibility to hold the entire institution "in trust," or they violate their oath. If they remain special interest board members, the rest of the body should, in the interest of service to all, help them realize their greater institutional responsibility or take whatever action is needed to have them removed.

Mary Follett summed up her discussion of power-with by stating:

> I should say that if we have any power, any genuine power, let us hold on to it, let us not give it away. We could not anyway if we wanted to. We can confer authority; but power or capacity, no man can give or take. The manager cannot share *his* power with division superintendents or foreman or worker, but he can give them opportunities for developing *their* power. Functions may have to be redistributed; something the manager does now had better perhaps be left to a division superintendent, to a foreman, even to a workman; but that is a different matter; let us not confuse the two things. Indeed, one of the aims of that very distribution of function should be how it can serve to evolve more power—more power to turn the wheels. More power, not division of power, should always be our aim; more power for the best possible furtherance of that activity, whatever it may be, to which we are giving our lives.[11]

Boards commit to represent the best interests of the college or university. Presidents commit to use their power to further the board's policy decisions. Faculty commit to provide the best they can by way of instructional excellence and worthwhile research and scholarship. We have chosen to give our lives to education and to the institutions that further its aims in our society. We will find the greatest success in that activity, and the greatest satisfaction for ourselves and those with whom we serve, by fostering the development of power for each person, and by supporting its use as a collective endeavor. The next chapter discusses how institutional goals can be realigned and power shared, while still furthering the needs and interests of all concerned.

NOTES

1. Paul Hersey and Kenneth H. Blanchard, *Management of Organizational Behavior* (Englewood Cliffs, NJ: Prentice-Hall, 1972), 32–33.

2. Alan Kolp and Peter Rea, *Leading with Integrity: Character-Based Leadership* (Cincinnati, OH: Atomic Dog Publishing, 2006), 64–66.

3. Gregory Moorhead and Ricky W. Griffith, *Organizational Behavior: Managing People and Organizations* (Boston: Houghton Mifflin, 1995), 328–329.

4. Robert K. Greenleaf, *On Becoming a Servant Leader*, ed. Don M. Frick and Larry Spears (San Francisco: Jossey-Bass, 1996), 129–139.

5. Stephen R. Covey, *Principle-Centered Leadership* (New York: Simon & Schuster, 1990), 101–103.

6. Sally Helgesen, "The Female Advantage," in *To Lead or Not To Lead* (Jackson, MS: Phi Theta Kappa, 1995), 1.35–1.36.

7. Warren Bennis, *Why Leaders Can't Lead* (San Francisco: Jossey-Bass, 1989), 72–73.

8. Robert K. Greenleaf, *Seeker and Servant: Reflections on Religious Leadership*, ed. Anne Fraker and Larry Spears (San Francisco: Jossey-Bass, 1996), 83.

9. Frederick Rudolph, *The American College & University: A History* (Athens: University of Georgia Press, 1990), 291.

10. John Carver, *Boards That Make a Difference: A New Design for Leadership in Nonprofit and Public Organizations* (San Francisco: Jossey-Bass, 2006).

11. Mary Parker Follett, *Mary Parker Follett: Prophet of Management*, ed. Pauline Graham (Boston: Harvard Business School Press, 1995), 115.

CHAPTER

Redesigning Higher Education

The time has come for addressing accumulated deficiencies. A highly educated population is essential if Americans are to be secure, healthy, and gainfully employed. The lesson of *Measuring Up 2004* is that higher education urgently requires a deliberate and renewed infusion of energy, commitment, and creativity.

—*Measuring Up 2004*

The quote above comes from introductory comments entitled "A Ten-year Perspective: Higher Education Stalled Despite High School Improvements," written by Patrick Callan for the *Measuring Up 2004* report. Callan follows the quote by stating, "Policy leadership by governors and legislators is essential. The educational and economic aspirations of individuals, the states, and the nation can be realized in the twenty-first century only through concerted and informed action."[1]

While some action by governors and legislatures may be required to address our "accumulated deficiencies," the higher education community will be better served if the changes are initiated by its leadership from within, with the advice and consent of its key constituents. The solutions are not new, but must be given renewed emphasis and energy. They will test the ingenuity, power, courage, and commitment to service of our best leadership. But I see no long-term solutions to the deficiencies referenced above without significant restructuring.

PREMIER TEACHING COLLEGES AND UNIVERSITIES

Beginning in the early 1970s, Charles McClain undertook a carefully planned and systematically executed series of steps that, over the next two decades, transformed Northeast Missouri State University (NMSU) into one of the most prominent public liberal arts colleges in the country. When McClain came to NMSU, he found a relatively nondescript regional college with a normal school history. When he left 17 years later, he and the rest of the university community had transformed this small, Midwestern college into a national leader in undergraduate achievement that, in 1995, formally became Truman State University.

McClain did not undertake this transformation in what many considered the most fertile academic setting. One of the oldest colleges west of the Mississippi, NMSU was located in rural Kirksville, Missouri, a relatively isolated farming community with a reputation for having some of the state's coldest weather. McClain brought to the university a belief that the public would respond positively to an institution that focused primarily on exceptional undergraduate learning. Finding in NMSU an institution with no clear sense of mission or direction when he arrived, he immediately began to exercise the principles of power-with.

In 1971, with an endorsement from the Faculty Senate's Planning and Development Committee, McClain formed the approximately 100-member Commission on Institutional Goals and Priorities for the Seventies, composed of faculty, administration, students, alumni, and friends of the university. The Truman State University Master Plan 1997–2007 reveals that, in addition, "McClain gently, but persistently, led the faculty into an examination of the university's performance and the quality of student learning that was occurring on campus. He believed that all higher education institutions had a positive obligation to assure that students actually received the high-quality educational experiences they expected when they enrolled."[2]

A series of recommendations emerged from the commission report, which have served as guiding principles for university planning and action since. The recommendations required that:

1. Standards of excellence in the structure and mode of learning and development be ascertained and maintained.

2. Each academic division formulate a plan to identify and measure the skills, knowledge, attitudes, and understandings which students should attain.

3. Prospective students be sought who have demonstrated excellence in ability and achievement.

4. Minimum requirements which can be externally measured be established for graduation.

5. A philosophical basis be developed for the common general educational requirements for the bachelor's degree.

6. Full recognition and support be given to the cultural aspects of university life in order to maintain excellence in this area.

7. Emphasis be placed on attracting many students from diverse cultural and social backgrounds to NMSU.[3]

As an employee participant-observer in this process, I watched as McClain skillfully crafted these recommendations into a series of administrative actions that gradually reshaped the institution into a model of undergraduate learning.

As new faculty were hired, applicants were recruited from the world's best universities—individuals who had themselves demonstrated academic prowess. McClain shared his vision with each, and explained that the university had made a commitment to recruit the best students it could attract and wanted these students to have the best teaching available. Faculty would be encouraged to do research and to publish, but first and foremost, they were to focus on excellence in instruction.

To attract students who would prosper in this aggressive academic environment, McClain developed a scholarship program that was, at the time, unrivaled in the state. In addition to having all educational costs covered, students receiving the Pershing Scholarship were inducted into the Pershing Society where they received special mentoring, supplementary seminars with distinguished visitors, and eventually a semester abroad experience paid for by the institution. Each year, admissions selectivity was edged upward, despite regular expressions of concern that it would hinder enrollment. The president's vision was not one of growth, but of academic excellence, and McClain favored a stable enrollment in which new resources were committed to improving the experience for each student, if that was the price for maintaining rigor.

Central to the entire vision was accountability—what McClain referred to as "value added." Each step in a student's progress was assessed—to the point that students complained that they couldn't walk across campus without being evaluated in some way. The elaborate assessment system included "in-process" measures to determine what was happening to students as they moved through the university and capstone evaluations to determine outcomes. Where subject-specific Graduate Records Exams were available, departments used them as exit assessments, and where they were not, other nationally normed measures were identified and employed.

Armed with this data, McClain went to the state legislature and convinced them to fund his vision; reward the university for its ability to show what students were learning—not based upon its capital development plan or on its enrollment projections, but based on evidence that the university was producing academic results. The strategy worked not only with the legislature, but also with the national media rating systems that have consistently listed Truman State as one of the best public university "buys" in the nation.[4]

Truman State's lessons to colleges and universities are clear and do not need to include increasingly selective admissions. To produce exceptional undergraduate teaching institutions, college leadership must:

- insist that what constitutes excellence in a degree program is clearly defined within each discipline—not by courses to be taken, but by knowledge, skills, and aptitudes to be gained;
- require that each discipline develop measures to evaluate these desired achievements;
- hire faculty as much for their excellence in teaching as for their research and scholarly credentials, and continuously develop and reward those skills;

- utilize capstone measures of overall achievement that are nationally normed, and have in place a review and continuous improvement system that feeds results back to departments and rewards them for revision and improvement;
- at some point in the process, whether at the capstone level or at an earlier stage of progress, include a "high stakes" assessment beyond which a student may not progress without demonstrating the minimum acceptable level of achievement.

I struggled for years over the advisability of this final requirement, but now realize that without it, we will never achieve what we need to as a nation to remain intellectually competitive. The concern has always been that few students will choose to impose this "achieve or else" requirement upon themselves, and will make other college choices to avoid it. I have decided that this will be true only if other choices exist, and if the benefits of the learning-centered curriculum are not seen as sufficiently enticing to encourage students or their parents to support the more rigorous choice.

As an undergraduate at Brigham Young University, I recall having to pass an English proficiency exam before advancing to junior status. Applicants knew that it was an expectation, but the other perceived values of attending the university were such that applications annually exceeded capacity. In this case, some of the perceived values were nonacademic, but colleges that establish a reputation for academic value can anticipate the same willingness to do what is necessary to take advantage of the exceptional so-called product the college or university offers.

There is an important lesson to be learned here from the nation's community colleges, which now uniformly require academic assessment of entering students and mandate remediation for identified deficiencies. Students have no choice—they take the developmental course, or they don't continue. The uniform requirement took nearly a century to develop across the system, but is now virtually universal in math and English. It works for two reasons: students have no other options, and they can try and try again until they get it right.

Community colleges are no better than four-year institutions in mandating minimum achievement levels for graduation, but beginning at the state level, colleges and universities could agree on requirements for junior-rising readiness or for graduation. If these standards were uniformly in place, we would immediately see the emergence of the "best value added" institutions as a category in national media ratings. Colleges could then gain the prestige they desire for being learning institutions and faculty the legitimacy that would make great teaching a desired career path. This transformation will be largely a matter of action by committed and courageous leadership.

UNDERGRADUATE EDUCATION AND RESEARCH UNIVERSITIES

University leaders, acting in their roles as public servants, must also reestablish undergraduate learning as having equal status with research in even our most prestigious research institutions—or must guide us through the difficult separation between institutes of pure research and those exclusively committed to teaching. Sperber suggests dividing "graduate programs into research training and undergraduate teaching tracks," with PhD candidates choosing to serve as teaching or research assistants.[5] My sense is that in the long term, divisions *within* universities will not work—assigning some faculty exclusively to instructional roles and others to research. Even if a system is developed that rewards teaching faculty at levels commensurate with their research colleagues, it will be virtually impossible to eliminate a class system based on a sense of disproportionate work load, access to funding sources, and resource allocation. Teaching faculty will inevitably become the academic underclass.

The clearer solution is to separate universities into teaching institutions, and graduate level/research institutes where faculty teach a graduate course or two and engage in research and publication, assisted by graduate students pursuing either a teaching or research track. The exclusively teaching institutions would have no need for graduate programs above the master's level, and would function much as Truman State University does, with some expected scholarship to keep faculty intellectually engaged in their disciplines, but with a primary focus on excellence in instruction. Faculty would be drawn from the graduate research institutes, from among those whose real love is the classroom, rather than the laboratory or archives.

The immediate question this proposal raises is, "But how do we fund the research, without the large undergraduate courses to generate support dollars?" The answers are simple, though perhaps unpalatable to many currently engaged in this pursuit.

1. Research institutes will have to depend on sponsored research, much as they do now, recognizing the accompanying ethical and directional issues that accompany sponsorship.

2. Institutes must rely on limited graduate tuition, state appropriations, federal grants, and foundation proposals to support the remainder of the research agenda. This reliance will force an accountability upon faculty for the amount and quality of the research being done, will greatly reduce both quantity and cost of academic research, and will apply a litmus test of "recognized value" to research projects.

If we can accomplish this division, the newly required accountability for research productivity will lead many to prefer the "teaching track," and we should have little difficulty attracting qualified faculty to our undergraduate learning universities.

What academic leader in his or her right mind is going to go to the Board of Regents and recommend that the university take to the legislature a recommendation that the University of California, Michigan, or Texas divide into two separate units or move purely to graduate status and leave undergraduate teaching and learning to another institution in the state? It will be the next Charles Eliot, who introduced broad-based academic choices to Harvard's curriculum, or William Rainey Harper, who fathered the community college and distance learning movements from his presidency at the University of Chicago. It will be another Charles McClain—a servant of education who chooses to be more than just a footnote in this century's academic record.

REDEFINING THE UNDERGRADUATE CURRICULUM

Suppose that each college leader who chooses to be less revolutionary was simply to assemble a 100-member commission similar to the one convened by Charles McClain and honestly seek its advice about what and how undergraduates should learn. Let us assume that we have a representative cross section of business and civic leadership, current and prospective students, and practitioners from secondary education and from the scientific community. For good measure, we add several nationally recognized specialists in teaching and learning to share their views about what is working in instructional design and learning methodologies. What would we hear?

I believe we can guess with some accuracy what the group would say, and would find that the commission has three values: it would confirm much of what we already know, suggest a few things we haven't considered, and legitimize the list of recommendations that emerges. It would provide leaders with the voices of the greater community to share in utilizing power for change. The list would look something like this:

1. *We are failing to prepare students for a globally integrated world by providing a domestic curriculum.* The business community would note that in late 2005, China passed the United States as the major manufacturing nation in the world, and at its current rate of economic growth, will have a standard of living equal to ours by 2031.[6] They would remind us that work is no longer place centered, and that multinational corporations no longer think in terms of brain drains and international outsourcing, because their perspective is global rather than purely American. Scientists in the group might ask if students are being challenged to think about the ecological consequences that China's standard of living could create if it equals our own by 2031—that if it mirrors our rate of energy consumption, we currently do not generate enough fossil fuel in the entire world to meet just its national demands.[7] And by then, with current growth rates, India will be the largest nation in the world, with an equally aggressive economy. These business and scientific leaders will ask why Roper survey data from a National Geographic study of 18–24-year-olds in nine countries indicated that:

   - only 25 percent of Americans polled could accurately place the population of the United States within 200 million—the poorest performance by students in any of the nine countries;
   - only 25 percent knew which two countries had populations over 1 billion—seventh of the nine;
   - more Canadians, Japanese, French, Mexicans, and Swedes could find the United States on a map than could Americans;

- American respondents were lowest in locating Russia, Japan, and Italy, and only 17 percent could select Afghanistan from four widely scattered choices;

- fifty-six percent of 3,000 Americans between 18 and 24 could not identify India from four widely scattered map choices.[8]

A bold representative from the international studies office might point out that national data indicate that only 1 percent of American college students study abroad—hardly the basis for a globally aware society![9] These members of our committee will ask why we are not doing more about the factors the Roper survey identified as influencing this poor performance—limited education in geography, modern language, travel and cultural studies, current events awareness, and internet use. They will wonder why we are not *requiring* geography, economics, and a second language—not so much to be able to communicate, but to assist with understanding.

2. *We are failing to prepare students to address the growing divide between the affluent and a burgeoning underclass who are undereducated, underemployed, and underproductive.* As baby boomers move into retirement, live longer, expect greater social support and health care, and as an undereducated population is left to fill the employment void and support growing social costs, are we requiring students to examine these serious social issues and grapple with solutions and consequences? Committee members from the social services sector will raise questions about how we plan to contribute to closing the knowledge and employability gap, while the learning specialists on our committee will point out that so-called service-learning appears to be an effective strategy for increasing volunteerism and raising social awareness, but is expected of very few.

3. *Faculty are often a generation behind students in their abilities to use technology effectively and in acknowledging it as a credible resource.* If confident that she won't be censured for speaking up, one of our students is likely to complain that her teachers don't know the first thing about technology. "We still sit through lectures that could easily be posted on a website, leaving us class time for discussion," she might offer. "Plus, I turned in an assignment the professor said had too many online journal citations. They were exactly the same journals we have in the library. I'm being negatively evaluated based on the professor's lack of familiarity with even the most basic knowledge of electronic resources." Students might also complain that the anytime/anywhere conveniences of distance learning classes are being challenged not so much on the data, which show them equally effective as learning methods, but because faculty don't want to trouble with the technology, are not comfortable converting their traditional delivery approaches into formats that work online, or do not want the additional workload of online instruction.

4. *We have a continuum of educational progression that is disjointed and poorly integrated.* Our K-12 partners will chide us for continuously complaining about the underpreparedness of high school graduates, yet doing very little to assist in bringing about change. Our faculties rarely, if ever, meet with their K-12 counterparts to review alignment of curricula, and when they do, it is often for each to indict the

other rather than to seek solutions. "We *understand* the problems," the secondary educators will say, "but we see little coming from you by way of solutions. Through your community colleges, you admit any student with a high school diploma or certificate, even if the grade report and test scores show underperformance, and you provide every opportunity to remediate. How one does in high school has absolutely nothing to do with whether one can get into *some* college. What motivation does that provide for students to achieve?" If they are feeling feisty, they may observe that colleges rarely have a minimum learning standard for graduation either, and are fortunate that no one is receiving our graduates and uniformly evaluating them for what they gained from their experience with us! While attending a conference in China sponsored by the International Finance Corporation of the World Bank, I was surprised to learn that senior IFC officials were quite critical of academic integration in the United States—what I had always viewed as the gold standard in articulation and transferability. "Perhaps once," one official told me, "when the concept was new. But little has changed in the United States in articulation in 25 years. You still make judgments about the quality of each other's offerings based on institutional type and departmental politics. That's not much of a model, as far as we're concerned. Others are passing you by."

5. *We know a great deal about what works well in learning, but don't use that knowledge.* Our out-of-town learning specialist will tell us that research is showing that students who are involved in collaborative learning activities show greater gains. When students teach one another, learning and retention are improved. Learning communities, where students take a series of courses together, study in groups, and serve as support systems to each other, compound the value of collaborative learning. These learning specialists will wonder why we know this, and yet are not insisting that all students become involved in learning communities of one kind or another.

6. *We are allowing entrenched, archaic procedures to drive decision making, even when we know the decisions are not in the best interests of the institution or our students.* One of our deans, no longer able to restrain herself, will wonder aloud why we still have an "evening college" or a "division of continuing education" that gets credit for anything offered after 4:00 P.M. or delivered online or off-campus. "I'm getting pressure to build enrollment, and the real opportunities are in distance learning," she will explain. "But all distance learning credit is attributed in the budget to Continuing Education! I am either faced with encouraging faculty to teach in a format that doesn't accommodate our new student interests, or with losing the credits taught by my own faculty to another administrative unit. This might have made sense when distance education was new and experimental—but that was 20 years ago. Isn't it time for an audit of our processes?"

From this commission—from our willingness to hear every voice—we would learn that:

1. We must analyze and revise curricula in every discipline to insure that each is relevant to today's global reality and focused so that students cannot graduate without appropriate international learning.

2. We must insure that the curriculum is also socially relevant, preparing students to grapple with the significant social and cultural problems of our age.

3. In a technological world, we must provide students with instruction that is as attuned to technological developments as are our students.

4. We must accept responsibility for assisting elementary and secondary education with improving the preparation of high school graduates.

5. It is time to create uniform standards for transfer and articulation, rather than leaving this to institutional whim and departmental protectionism.

6. We must hire and train faculty who can teach utilizing instructional methods that are proven to improve student learning.

7. We must conduct audits of our operational processes to insure that they make administrative sense.

These are the challenges facing the college leader committed to service to all. Critical to meeting each is the need to establish a level of organizational trust that allows those inside the institution to feel that change is occurring with their interests in mind, and those outside to recognize that they have had a voice in shaping the new direction.

NOTES

1. Patrick M. Callan, "A Ten-year Perspective: Higher Education Stalled Despite High School Improvements," *Measuring Up 2004 Report*, National Center for Public Policy and Higher Education: 2005, 8.

2. Truman State University, "Chapter II: History of Assessment at Truman State University," in *Truman State University Master Plan* (Kirksville, MO: Truman State University 1997–2007/May 30 version), II-1, http://www.truman.edu/userfiles/academics/masterplan.pdf.

3. Ibid., II-2.

4. Truman State University Web site, "What Makes Truman Amazing," Truman State University, http://www.truman.edu/pages/199.asp.

5. Murray Sperber, "How Undergraduate Education Became College Lite," in *Declining by Degrees: Higher Education at Risk*, ed. Richard H. Hersh and John Merrow (New York: Palgrave Macmillan, 2005), 141–142.

6. Lester R. Brown, *Plan B 2.0: Rescuing a Planet Under Stress and a Civilization in Trouble* (New York: W. W. Norton, 2006), 10.

7. Ibid..

8. National Geographic Education Foundation, "National Geographic—Roper 2002 Global Geographic Literacy Survey," November 2002, http://www.nationalgeographic.com/geosurvey/download/RoperSurvey.pdf.

9. David L. Wheeler, "More Students Study Abroad, but Their Stays Are Shorter," *Chronicle of Higher Education*, 17 November 2000, A74.

CHAPTER

Trust and Consensus during Change

Trust is the lubrication that makes it possible for organizations to work.
—Warren Bennis

The kind of collaborative exercise of power discussed in Chapter Eight and
the aggressive change agenda covered in the last chapter simply are not
possible without *trust*—a trust that by virtually any leader's admission is
difficult to achieve. It is a trust that must begin with the leader and defines one
of the most challenging responsibilities of the person who wishes to be a change
agent: to be completely trustworthy. Katherine Tyler Scott, in her contributing
chapter to *Spirit at Work*, writes about power-with organizations, and notes that:
"Trust is foundational to the health and survival of any organization, and creating
and maintaining this trust is the responsibility of the leader."[1] If power within an
organization during a period of transition is to be exercised as power-with, trust is
the critical ingredient and it must be shared by all stakeholders.

In *Driving Fear Out of the Workplace*, Kathleen Ryan and Daniel Oestreich cite
some of the early writing of the new so-called science of management that emerged
in the decades of the 50s and 60s, in which students of the emerging discipline
noted the relationship between distrust and fear. Douglas McGregor observed that
effective communication, which he viewed as a foundation to effective management, depended upon "a climate of mutual trust and support with the group. In
such a climate, members can be themselves without fear of consequences."[2] Jack
Gibb, writing somewhat later, commented on the cyclical nature of the distrust-
fear relationship, observing that distrust breeds fear, which in turn creates even
greater distrust, until all internal relationships are destroyed.[3]

Yet blind trust, Greenleaf observed, is as dangerous as distrust. He believed there to be an *optimum* trust that lies somewhere between distrust and blind faith in the leader. It is an informed trust based upon tested experience with each other, a trust that is always fragile, but can become strong enough to weather momentary lapses once all involved come to know that the core trust is genuine.

The recipe for this kind of trust is complex with dozens of ingredients, some more essential than others, but all contributing to the whole. Several are particularly important and deserve brief elaboration, recognizing that each leader will have personal additions.

DEMONSTRATE GENUINE CARING

No ingredient is more critical to trust than genuinely caring about those with whom you work and about the organization for which you work. Leadership is an act of love—for the institution, and for those who work to make it successful. When leaders find it difficult to get along with some people with whom they must work closely, Follett's Law of the Situation model provides the means to address these differences by allowing each to say, "There is a conflict between us that needs to be worked out so we can work effectively together. Let's see what is at the root of the difference, and it will suggest what we need to do to improve our relationship."

In a later chapter on barriers to service, I suggest that caring for others must be demonstrated in overt ways, but want to emphasize here that the demonstration *must* be genuine. The leader must be able to laugh and share joy with the happy moments others experience and weep with their sorrows—always because there is genuine concern for, and interest in, their lives.

PARTICIPATE

Some management books suggest that leaders spend time in one of the line positions periodically, getting a feel for what workers are doing. I would go a step farther by suggesting that academic leadership should constantly be engaged in the central activity of the enterprise—teaching and learning. Every administrator with the background to do so should teach and, if at the research university level, remain actively engaged in scholarly writing or research. This is necessary partly to remain intellectually vital and partly to remain engaged in the important conversations and activities of the institution. Each should periodically attend faculty meetings within his or her discipline and participate in department or divisional planning discussions. When rosters and grades are due, the president's grades and rosters should be in. This kind of scholarly involvement will contribute as much to a sense of power-with and trust as will any other college commitment.

Some presidents will maintain that, with other time demands, they cannot commit to teaching. Many of these same leaders continue their involvement in research and writing, however, reinforcing the institutional view of research as a higher priority. But online, evening, and weekend courses, hybrid seminars, and team teaching opportunities mean that any college leader who wishes to can remain involved in instruction during at least one term per year. Follett wrote of the effective leader: "In every way, he must show that he is willing to do what he urges on others."[4] (Follett would, I'm sure, have been more gender sensitive if writing today!)

Remaining involved in the teaching life of the institution is only half of the "pedagogical participation" equation in the academic community. The other half is learning. In an earlier chapter, I noted Peter Vaill's observation that the rapid rate of change in virtually all aspects of professional life has created a condition that he equates to rafting on a river of perpetual white water. Because of this magnitude of change, he equates today's management process with "what we are like when we are playing a game we have never played before, for that is what permanent white water creates: an environment of continual newness."[5] As a result, organizational knowledge and leadership understanding are also in a constant state of change, requiring continuous learning by those involved in the leadership process. Vaill maintains that "management leadership is not learned; management leadership is learning. Permanent white water has made learning the preeminent requirement of all managerial leadership, beyond all of the other characteristics and requisite competencies."[6]

One might argue with Vaill's preeminent claim, but he is certainly right in maintaining that, unless a leader is viewed by others in the organization as being a constant learner, a student of change and its effects on the organization, it will be difficult to engender trust. A great deal more will be said about the importance of continual learning in Chapter Twelve.

LISTEN TO CRITICISM

Leaders must be open to bad news. In fact, they must develop an atmosphere that encourages it to come to their attention. Few things are more destructive to trust than rumor or discontent that is allowed to fester beneath the surface. One must believe in the Law of the Situation, get issues out in the open, and deal with them objectively and fairly, even if the leader is the object of the criticism. When others in the organization learn that they can come to you with concerns and criticisms and receive a fair hearing, it will add immeasurably to building trust.

Many CEOs suffer from what might be called the "last to know" syndrome, hearing criticism and bad news only after it has circulated completely through the institution. There is no simple way to establish an earlier position in the information loop, but in many ways, the process is just a matter of reversing the "fear/mistrust" cycle. Trust fosters earlier notification of difficulties, and careful handling of criticism encourages greater trust. As with each element of trust building, as others learn that the leader is always trying to do "what is right," trust will follow.

INFORM

My experience as a president was that it is impossible for the leader to pass along too much valid information, particularly to the governing board, but also to faculty and staff. They will occasionally complain, "We don't need to know all this," but are also inclined to believe something is being hidden from them that might be important if all information is not shared.

Explain what is happening in the legislature that might affect funding. Relate the deliberations of the state presidents' association, as long as they are not viewed as confidential. Share information from national conferences that might be of interest, and pass along any internal successes, problems, or issues, as long as they do not compromise a confidentiality. And above all, share your vision of the future, especially of those areas where change seems inevitable.

Following Air Force pilot training during the Vietnam conflict, I spent two weeks in Spokane, Washington, going through the service's survival school. Part of the training included a simulated prisoner of war (POW) experience that involved capture, incarceration, interrogation, mild mistreatment, and two sleepless days of continuous discomfort. One participant found himself to be so claustrophobic that confinement in the small boxes we were locked in for periods of time was intolerable, and he fell apart. His shouting brought immediate relief, but was so disturbing to others that during the critique at the end of the simulated POW experience, several participants asked if all the torment had been necessary.

The sergeant directing the exercise explained that they had learned from the few POWs who had returned from Vietnam by that time that the more closely they had simulated the experiences of captivity prior to actually being captured, the less traumatic the real experience turned out to be.

"These returning POWs tell us," the sergeant explained, "that when they found themselves in a situation like the boxes, they would say to themselves, 'I've been here before and know I can deal with this.' So we try to let you know in advance exactly what you might be exposed to. Much of fear is not knowing what to expect."

The same is true of anticipating institutional change. Fear develops, in part, from not knowing what to expect. The more clearly the leader is able to project an image of that future, the less fear will be a factor as anticipated developments become realities.

Experienced leaders know that when options related to a pending decision are discussed and shared openly, some are inclined to react to each option as if it is the final decision, even if the option is one of the weaker choices. Gradually, this reactionism diminishes as people begin to understand that the organization will work through options and discuss a final decision before it is set in stone—or in motion.

All criticism, whether directed at the leader or at others, is not necessarily merited, yet the invitation to express it is often seen as an indication that "something will be done about it." Sharing information includes the necessity on occasion to let individuals expressing criticism know that the concerns have been evaluated as objectively as possible but were not found to be legitimate.

CREDIT FREELY/BLAME SLOWLY

Consider your own experience and how irritating (and trust breaking) it was when you were not credited with one of your ideas or efforts that proved particularly successful. Remember, also, those occasions when blame was directed your way for a failure or mistake that either was not yours or over which you had little control. Jim Collins's level 5 leaders were those who were willing to assume responsibility for what went wrong, and who widely dealt out praise and credit to others for the organization's successes.[7]

To lead effectively, you do *not* have to take credit for every success. Most, in fact, will not be your doing, but will result from the work of many. One of the most common "trust-breakers" is the effort of supervisors to take credit for another's work and ideas—a breach of trust that rarely escapes notice by the offended person and by others in the work area.

Similarly, most failures and mistakes are also shared efforts, are immediately recognized by those responsible, and become much more destructive if immediately called to general attention. It helps to place failure or error in perspective by realizing what great teachers they can be to the person or persons involved and to the institution as a whole. Edison is credited with having pointed out to an assistant who was lamenting the fact that hundreds of substances had failed to produce a suitable light filament that he should think instead of how much they now knew about what did not work.

There are, of course, occasions in which someone makes a foolish or costly blunder that must be corrected immediately. If it is intentional or dishonest, appropriate action needs to be taken. But in most cases, error is best addressed through a private evaluation of what happened, what the result was, and what can be learned from the experience—all without minimizing the effects of the mistake. Unless a problem is an emergency, it is often best not to react immediately. When a situation first comes to light, the leader rarely knows what needs to be known to contribute to the best decision. Taking the time to get the right information avoids mistakenly affixing blame or responding inappropriately, thereby compounding the error.

The importance of reviewing mistakes privately can't be overemphasized. I recall an administrative retreat for a leadership team during which we talked about the elements of "team" that each member particularly valued in our working relationship. We decided that we would benefit from signing an agreement outlining specific tenets by which we would work together. Among these were to respect and value each team member, to disagree agreeably, and to give team members the benefit of the doubt. By this last item, we meant that if something didn't appear to be going smoothly, we would get together privately and talk about it before taking other action. Trust results from knowing that if one tries and succeeds, recognition will come with the success. If one fails while doing one's best, there will be opportunities to try again.

BE CALM, UPBEAT, AND POSITIVE

One of my early mentors never failed to impress me when faced with a crisis by listening to the situation almost without expression, thinking about what he had heard for a few minutes, then calmly stating, "Well, let's see what we need to do to get this taken care of." His ability to consider what I thought to be even the most troubling news with calm thoughtfulness engendered as much confidence in his leadership as did the eventual resolution to the problem. It is a skill that can be developed with practice, but should not be confused with immobility or inaction in times of crisis. It simply requires a few moments of careful thought, followed by action.

I am constantly reminded of the three-step emergency procedure that was drummed into my head as a student pilot. "Maintain aircraft control. Analyze the situation. Take proper action." The few critical emergencies that I experienced while flying taught me that steps one and two are just as critical as step three. The steps might be rephrased to recommend: (1) Maintain self-control, control of the institutional environment, and of the emotions of others faced with the crisis. (2) Analyze the situation. (3) Take proper action. The result will be greater trust and confidence in the leadership being exhibited.

A similar skill relates to how the leader deals with the routine stresses of the job. For each person who leads an organization of any size or complexity, there are days—sometimes weeks—of relentless pressure and stress. They arise from troubling personnel issues, from financial uncertainties, from the wearing effects of long days spent testifying before legislative committees. To maintain the level of confidence and trust needed to keep the institution running smoothly, these pressures and stresses must remain largely invisible. They can be shared with a spouse or partner, or perhaps with an assistant in whom the leader has complete faith and confidence, but otherwise, they remain the leader's burden. The leader's public persona during these times needs to be positive and upbeat. The same mentor who always exhibited calm in the face of crisis commented to me, when he learned that I was assuming a presidency, "There are some times when you will need to be lonely. Be ready for them and see them as part of the job."

BE ETHICAL

Trust, to a large degree, depends on the perception that the person in whom trust is being placed will always make the best effort to do what is right. A board member whom I greatly admire is a retailer who often deals in traded and used equipment. On occasion, a buyer, often a good friend, will offer to pay for a piece of used equipment with cash, noting with a wink that the payment may then not have to show up as income. During a conversation on ethics, the board member mentioned these offers and explained why he always refuses. "In addition to being dishonest," he said, "it would send a message, even to the friend who is encouraging it, that I am not completely ethical in my dealings with others. Though he might wink at this occurrence, he can't help but wonder if I am equally unethical in the way I overhaul and price what I am selling to him."

I am often dismayed at how readily people in leadership positions compromise ethics to legality. A school board in a community where I worked for many years refused to adopt a nepotism policy because "there was no legal requirement to do so," then immediately followed the inaction by hiring the wife of one of its members to fill a responsible district position. The faculty committee that had interviewed candidates for the position had not included the spouse on its list of finalists, and her selection destroyed any element of trust the employees had in their board. What is legal is not always what is right, and ethics is a matter of rightness, not of legality. Francis Hesselbein writes: "Leaders model desired behaviors, never break a promise, and know that leadership is a matter of how to be, not how to do it."[8]

In an environment in which power, decision making, and trust are to be shared, ethical decisions and behavior should be expected of everyone. Otherwise power-with will lose much of its appeal to those who do not trust others to do what is right. Mary Follett wrote:

> The single most important characteristic may well be a willingness to tell the truth. In a world of growing complexity and speed (some call it "raplexity"), leaders are increasingly dependent on their subordinates for good information, whether they want to hear it or not. Followers who tell the truth and leaders who listen to it are an unbeatable combination.[9]

BE ACCESSIBLE

Perhaps this trust-builder should have been listed first, since it is essential to the success of many of the others. People are hesitant to trust, confide in, or share with those they don't know. Granted, there are the innumerable other demands on a leader's time mentioned earlier, but if the leader is to build trust, it will come from spending time with people. Accessibility must include access to the soul as well as to the office. It includes being intimate with certain thoughts and beliefs—a willingness to say, "This is important to me because…" with the rest of the answer telling the colleague something about who the leader is and what affects the leader at his or her core. List those in whom you have the greatest trust and see what the common denominators are. One will be that it is a list of your "intimate" acquaintances, those who have given you access to their hearts and souls and to whom you have extended the same. Opening the soul is much more difficult than opening the office door. It requires a willingness to be personally vulnerable that many of us find uncomfortable. Yet it is key to establishing lasting trust.

WORK WITH SPIRIT

Jay Conger, in *Spirit at Work*, defines spirituality as "a selfless sense of love and compassion for others, respect and concern for well-being and life, and reverence for the universe and its creation."[10] Note that Conger does not say "creator," and his definition suggests that experience can be spiritual without being "religious."

In their work, *Leaders*, Warren Bennis and Burt Nanus note that "by focusing attention on a vision, the leader operates on the emotional and spiritual resources of the organization, on its values, commitment, and aspirations."[11] I would go even farther to say that true vision *depends* on those spiritual resources, on a sense of what should and can be. It depends on a communal understanding of what the institution and those within it can do to contribute to the universal well-being Conger mentions. It transcends the commonplace and routine and forces the question, "What do we exist for if we don't contribute in some significant way to the well-being of others?"

For the academic organization, that contribution may be through heightening understanding of the world and the human condition, through research that adds to that understanding, and through direct contribution of services that improve and strengthen society. Unless we deeply believe that what we do makes life better or improves the world in some important way, we work without purpose. This final element of leadership and trust building relates very closely to the first mentioned: genuine caring. It is the element of *belief* in leadership; belief in the goodness of what we do, and in the essential contribution made by the organization to perpetuation of that goodness. When the belief is genuine, it will be recognized and respected by those we serve.

For me, spirit in work has a much more personal dimension that is also critical to trust building. In the late 1980s, my wife and I spent a few days in a small group seminar conducted by Parker Palmer. Palmer, like Robert Greenleaf, has had deep connections with the Quaker community and draws from the quiet introspection of Quaker life for much of his thought. As a result, he sees spirituality in leadership in a much more personal and introspective way, encouraging those in leadership positions (and all people, for that matter,) to look inward for greater understanding of who and why we are what we are. I found Palmer's approach to be refreshingly free of psychological jargon and formulaic analysis. He simply encouraged us to look inward at what we feared, what our personal anxieties were and our senses of inadequacy, then consider how we might be using those as the basis for our own prejudices, suspicions, distrusts, and refusals to "attempt." To be able to fully trust and be trusted, Palmer maintains that we must first grapple with these shadows within.

This introspection also invites us to evaluate what is truly important to us. What makes us who we are and has brought us to where we are? When we have been gone for 50 years, what difference will it have made that we were here at all? Again, we begin to see the importance of transcending the commonplace and the routine, and committing ourselves to bettering the human condition. This is spirit at work.

CONSENSUS BUILDING

There is clearly more to adopting a power-with approach to leadership than establishing trust among those involved. The organization must be so ordered as to encourage the free flow of thoughts, concerns, and ideas, and must be structured in such a way that all are not only allowed, but encouraged to participate. One of the great attractions of Greenleaf's Servant-Leadership model is the approach he takes to this process. He generally rejects the concept of democratic governance, in the sense that issues should be "voted on." Voting, he points out, creates both winners and losers, and when the vote is close, there can be a number of losers! Instead, he envisions the leader-as-servant working in a consensus environment, but with a qualified definition of consensus. Rather than consensus being "full agreement by all concerned," Greenleaf sees it as that position where participants "either accept the position as the right or best one, or they agree to support it as a feasible resolution of the issue, being aware of the limited time for deliberation that may be allocated to any one issue."[12]

Jim Tatum, mentioned earlier as a nationally recognized college trustee, was a serious student of Greenleaf's and, for a time, chaired the Board of Directors of the Greenleaf Center. He decided that he needed to better understand the Quaker roots upon which Greenleaf drew and received permission to participate in a training session for "clerks" held at the Quaker community of Old Chatham. In the Society of Friends, the clerk is the person who conducts religious services and facilitates community meetings at which issues of importance are discussed and problems resolved. Following the experience, Jim shared with me two valuable lessons gathered from his week in Old Chatham.

The first was an appreciation for the power of silence—for the ability to sit for long periods of time without feeling the need to speak. Many of the Friends' meetings are punctuated by times during which no one speaks at all. These periods of contemplation allow each to consider, evaluate, and meditate, either on the topic being addressed, or on whatever the participant feels he or she needs to think about. They also encourage each member to focus more directly on what is said, once someone chooses to speak, rather than spending that time developing a response or personal view.

The second great lesson from the clerking session was a deeper understanding of the Friends' approach to consensus building, one that is particularly useful to power-with leadership. Using this approach, an issue is discussed until there seems to be broad general agreement with a solution, at which point the clerk asks, "Does anyone object to this solution strongly enough to feel that he/she should stand in the way of us moving forward?" If a person does object that strongly, the issue is revisited until a solution is found which is free of these objections.[13]

The process can be time consuming, but generally is not. As The Law of the Situation indicates, the solution is generally present in the facts surrounding the issue. The responsibility is well expressed by Follett in her statement that, "Out of a welter of facts, experiences, desires, aims, the leader must find the unifying thread. He must see a whole, not a mere kaleidoscope of pieces."[14] In helping to shape the issue, the leader both facilitates the speed of the process and directs it toward the institutional vision and goals.

This consensus-building model also provides an element of protection. It allows the leader to be among those who can express sufficient concern with the solution to impede its implementation. Since the leader is going to hold ultimate responsibility for the success of the solution, there obviously will be occasions when there is not the comfort level needed to assume that responsibility. On those occasions the leader can say, "I can't live with this," and the solution is revisited.

In an article originally published in *Fortune* magazine and republished in a collection of essays on Greenleaf's work, *Fortune* managing editor, Walter Kiechel III, observes that "the process works more like the consensus building that the Japanese are famous for. Yes, it takes a while on the front end; everyone's view is solicited though everyone also understands that his or her view may not ultimately prevail. But once the consensus is forged, watch out: With everyone on board, your so-called implementation proceeds wham-bam."[15] The challenge, of course, is to foster an environment and to structure an organization in such a way that this kind of consensus building can occur. Creating that environment requires that college leadership ensures that higher education retain one of its critically unique functions in society, to serve as a forum for the free expression of ideas. Insuring that freedom is the focus of the next chapter.

NOTES

1. Katherine Tyler Scott, "Leadership and Spirituality: A Quest for Reconciliation," in *Spirit at Work,* ed. Jay A. Conger (San Francisco: Jossey-Bass, 1994), 80–81.

2. Douglas McGregor, *The Professional Manager* (New York: McGraw-Hill, 1967), 192, as cited in Kathleen D. Ryan and Daniel K. Oestreich, *Driving Fear Out of the Workplace* (San Francisco: Jossey-Bass, 1991), 14–15.

3. Jack R. Gibb, *Trust* (Los Angeles: Guild of Tutors Press, 1978), as cited in Kathleen D. Ryan and Daniel K. Oestreich, *Driving Fear Out of the Workplace*, 14–15.

4. Mary Parker Follett, *Mary Parker Follett: Prophet of Management,* ed. Pauline Graham (Boston: Harvard Business School Press, 1995), 174.

5. Peter B. Vaill, *Learning as a Way of Being* (San Francisco: Jossey-Bass, 1996), xiv.

6. Ibid., 126.

7. James Collins, *Good to Great* (New York: HarperCollins, 2001), 35.

8. Francis Hesselbein, "Journey to Transformation," *Leader to Leader* 7 (1998): 7.

9. Follett, 179.

10. Jay A. Conger, introduction to *Spirit at Work* (San Francisco: Jossey-Bass, 1994), 12.

11. Warren Bennis and Burt Nanus, *Leaders* (New York: Harper & Row, 1985), 92.

12. Robert K. Greenleaf, *On Becoming a Servant Leader,* ed. Don M. Frick and Larry C. Spears (San Francisco: Jossey-Bass, 1996), 140–141.

13. James B. Tatum, personal communication with author.

14. Mary Parker Follett, *Freedom and Co-ordination: Lectures in Business Organization by Mary Parker Follett,* ed. L. Urwick (London: Management Publications Trust, Ltd., 1949), 52.

15. Walter Kiechel III, "The Leader as Servant," in *Reflections on Leadership,* ed. Larry C. Spears (New York: John Wiley & Sons, 1995), 123–124.

CHAPTER 11

Organizing for Service

I've learned that the most effective way to forge a winning team is to call on the players' need to connect with something larger than themselves.

—Phil Jackson

One aspect of Robert Greenleaf's use of Hermann Hesse's account of Leo in *Journey to the East* has always troubled me. Even though Leo's service provided leadership for the travelers, once he left the group, it disintegrated. The implication was that Leo's service and leadership were so tied to Leo, that the group could not function in his absence. Somehow, this falls short of great leadership. Great leadership not only provides direction and support, but builds within the group the ability to either find effective new leadership when a leader moves on, or become self-directing. Mary Follett continuously maintains in her writing that it is the responsibility of leaders to train followers to be leaders, reminiscent of Lao-Tzu's counsel that, "Of a good leader, who talks little, when his work is done, his aim fulfilled, they will all say, 'We did this ourselves.'"[1]

The ultimate responsibility of twenty-first century academic leadership is to shape an institution that can begin to think of itself as an organic whole, creating a sense of the institution as community leader. For community colleges, this role may extend no farther than to the community in which the college is located, while universities might have much broader national or international roles. There is no question that great universities have, in the past, distinguished themselves as national leaders, but most have done so largely though academic innovation—by introducing new curricular models or by pioneering delivery systems—rather than as instruments of social change. Pressures toward racial integration, gender equity, and ecological responsibility have been largely thrust upon us, in some cases with considerable resistance. With the exception of the community college movement and its emphasis on affordable access, few social initiatives of national proportion have received impetus from the academy. Some might argue that the antiwar movement during the Vietnam conflict was college initiated, but having been of draft age during that time, I would argue that the movement was less an institutional one than a response by students of draft age. Absent the draft, no such movement developed during the Iraq war of the first decade of this century.

If we think of the institution as an organism, perhaps we have found it difficult to serve as leaders for social, economic, and cultural change because we are not organic wholes. We are, as one colleague observed, "a loose confederation of dispirit interests." The left hand rarely knows what the right hand is doing, and often would just as soon not know. But if our nation is to provide responsible direction to its citizens and to others in this century, it is incumbent upon leadership in higher education to bring us together as organizational wholes, to foster and support service roles that target and aggressively confront our most intractable and destructive social, ecological, economic, and cultural ills.

Leadership in industry, sparked by quality circles and the "horizontal organization" revolution in management theory, has been fostering team-centered working relationships at such breakneck speed that it is often difficult to keep abreast of the latest developments in participatory involvement. The American academic community, though the purveyor of much of this theory, has been much less inclined to put it into practice. During the heyday of Total Quality Management (TQM), several colleges in the country experimented with academic models that incorporated TQM principles and offered workshops on the techniques. But the movement passed by most of the Ivory Tower without disturbing much of the foliage. There have been awkward attempts at *forcing* participatory governance, such as California's Shared Governance legislation, but legislating teamwork is much like legislating morality. Without the proper spirit, it becomes a new autocracy, with a few brandishing power-over based on the new moral code. It lacks the two ingredients that make teamwork *teamwork*—trust and a willingness to give up something personally to achieve a collective greater good. The complete quote from Chicago Bull's coach Phil Jackson that begins this chapter says:

> Most leaders tend to view leadership as a social engineering project: take group x, add y motivational technique and get z result. But working with the Bulls I've learned that the most effective way to forge a winning team is to call on the players' need to connect with something larger than themselves. Even for those who don't consider themselves "spiritual" in the conventional sense, creating a successful team—whether it's an NBA champion or a record-setting sales force—is essentially a spiritual act. It requires the individuals involved to surrender their self-interest for the greater good so that the whole adds up to more than the sum of its parts.[2]

It is this *spirit* that marks true cooperation and teamwork, a spirit based on a sense of mutual respect, common desire to achieve a goal, and appreciation for the fact that each person involved brings unique strengths to the partnership that combine to create a stronger whole. For various reasons, members of the higher education community have historical assumptions, practices, and protections that challenge the creation of an effective organic whole. If we are to assume roles as institutional agents of social change—as servants beyond the institution—our first responsibility is to tackle the demons within.

HIGHER EDUCATION AS BUREAUCRACY

Along with the military and branches of government, higher education is among the most hierarchical organizations in our society. We have presidents, chancellors, provosts, vice-everythings, deans, department chairs, full professors, associate professors, assistants, affiliates, and lecturers. And that is before we get to the support positions where additional vice-everythings supervise directors, supervisors, coordinators, and so forth. Our obsession with hierarchy is such a fact of organizational life that it is a favorite target of cartoonists in trade publications such as the *Chronicle of Higher Education*. Humor is often funny because it so closely mirrors unspoken truth, and two *Chronicle* cartoons are cases in point, poking fun at our awareness of the depth and caste nature of professorial rank. One depicted an official standing beside an easel, going over the four faculty ranking levels with a group of underlings. On the windowsill, one bird is saying to the other, "I think he's explaining their place in the food chain."[3] Another showed a faculty member saying to an administrator: "Sir, I regret to inform you that the faculty has mounted a 'How many vice-provosts does it take to screw in a light bulb' Web site."[4] Ironically, on the same page that displayed this last cartoon, a letter to the editor was signed by an individual using "Executive Assistant to the Vice-President, Director, Office of International Studies, and Professor of English" as his titles.

Writing about institutional transformation in the Drucker Foundation's publication, *Leader to Leader*, editor Francis Hesselbein lists eight milestones in transformational leadership. High on her list is, "Ban the Hierarchy." Hesselbein notes that "transformation requires moving people out of their organizational boxes into flexible, fluid management systems," noting that workers in today's knowledge-based work environment "carry their tools in their heads" and should not be constrained or restrained by highly structured work settings.[5] Curiously, while being a loose confederation of dispirit interests, the university is at the same time a highly structured one—with each dispirit interest wanting check-and-balance control over every decision, where even a change in course title can require five or six levels of approval.

In addition to stifling communication, this hierarchy essentially creates a class system that is in most ways artificial. Academic rank generally is based on level of education, time within the system, and to some measure, scholarship. But the evaluative criteria for scholarship are often quantitative rather than qualitative. Teaching effectiveness and other measures of direct service to students and the external community often are either not included in determining academic rank or carry little weight. When considering publications for faculty advancement, the substance and quality of the writing are judged less important than the ability of the author to get the piece published in one of the myriad "juried" journals, many of which exist primarily to provide outlets for this material. We have created a synthetic society that we refer to as collegial, but which is essentially a power-over system in which we compare ourselves to each other on a "greater than" or "less than" scale—the antithesis of a service-centered culture.

Academic organizations often remind me of a colonel I knew in the Air Force who hated to leave the base because, once beyond the main gate, no one acknowledged his rank or cared about what or who he was. He stayed on base whenever possible where the eagles on his shoulders garnered respect and status, where he had a special parking spot and name plate announcing his position, and where virtually everyone had to salute when he passed.

We have created our own closed society in which we expect the old military adage "rank has its privileges" to apply. Generations of students have had to review, sometimes seriously, sometimes in jest, how long they should wait for a professor who isn't there for the beginning of a class. "Now let's see, is that 15 minutes for a full professor and 10 for an associate? And what is old Dr. So-and-So anyway?" The more important questions should be, "Why is the professor late in the first place and what right does he or she have to waste the time and money of 30 to several hundred students who are paying a great deal of money for that time and expecting something worthwhile in return?" Beyond the campus, few in the general public know or care about the differences between professor, associate professor, assistant, affiliate, or lecturer. As far as they are concerned, you are simply a professor at the university with a responsibility to teach effectively.

I have generally been a critic of tenure, convinced that it has outlived its usefulness and now serves more to protect weakness than to ensure strength. Academic freedom is generally guaranteed in other policy or contractual agreements, and far more faculty abuse the essentially untouchable status provided by tenure than need its protection because they speak out on controversial issues. But in recent years, I have had a change of heart. Troubled by the dearth of voices that challenge public policy and societal absolutists, I have decided that tenure is still needed—but faculty need to be doing more to require its protection.

WHY TENURE?

In many ways, the free exchange of ideas is more tightly restricted inside the academy than it is in most other areas of public life. Inside the university community, one does not talk freely about issues related to race, gender, sexual orientation, or poverty. One talks appropriately about them—and to do otherwise invites being ostracized from the community. A president of Harvard can lose his job by failing to be circumspect about a comment made about gender, even when made in a forum created to explore related possibilities. Colleges and universities are, in fact, seats of power for political correctness. To need tenure—to merit it—faculty must begin again to publicly challenge the untouchable ideas and need the support and protection of administrations and boards to do so. And this so-called speaking out must extend *well* beyond scholarly journals and papers presented at esoteric academic convocations. It must occur in the places where average citizens gather—in our public schools, in town meetings, and on editorial pages in local papers. Faculty need to again *merit* tenure—because if the academic community does not foster public debate about issues of vital importance, no one will.

Politics have become too partisan to speak honestly about critical public issues. We have known for decades that the social security system is headed for bankruptcy, and know that politicians won't touch it. When they speak about key foreign policy issues, we can pretty closely script, based on political party, what they will say.

The politicians are not alone. We know that we are headed towards a series of environmental disasters if we fail to alter our behaviors as a nation and world, but the national media choose not to debate the issues in any significant way. The bulk of public consumption media is driven by revenues to be noncontroversial, and is largely pap. We worry that sponsored research is limiting the voices in the academy, while sponsored politics has quieted political dissent, and sponsored media have neutered the news of criticism and meaningful commentary.

Unfortunately, public colleges, and to some degree, independent ones, are subject to the same revenue pressures from patrons, legislatures, or governors who get upset about statements made by college personnel that are too controversial—too confrontational. But again, if the academic community is not publicly testing the ideas and decisions that are driving society, who will? Leadership in the new century, to properly serve, must foster and protect an environment in which universities again function as the public's conscience, and where tenure is again sorely needed.

But tenure should be maintained and protected only if it serves this purpose. Few, if any other, professions enjoy the protections tenure provides. It was created with justifiable cause—to insure that those who participated in the open marketplace of ideas are not censured for promoting thoughts that run contrary to commonly accepted orthodoxy. It guards against judgments of a dose of hemlock when the teachings of a Socrates provoke the ire of a senate. It allowed important revolutions and evolutions in thought to be heard. But where are these happening today? For the most part, tenure now serves to protect that small group of faculty which is minimally productive, but does little to further controversial debate.

Richard Tarnus's *Passion of the Western Mind* reminds us that most of the significant developments in our ethics, theory, and philosophy came from the unprotected—from people who were themselves intellectual revolutionaries and suffered considerably as a result. Lack of tenure did not keep them from espousing their ideas, nor has its existence during the last century made the difference between the presentation or suppression of bold new thought. In fact, as with academic rank, qualifications for tenure often seem to be more quantitative than qualitative. Another *Chronicle* cartoon aptly showed an academic seated at a computer entering the first lines of his next piece of work; "'A Modest Contribution to the Field. But Probably Enough to Get Me Tenure.' Chapter 1. Page 1."[6]

Tenure now needs to be exercised with purpose, and must become subject to periodic review by an objective panel of evaluators. On the limiting and obstructive side, it introduces an element of imbalance into the power-with equation. When the Law of the Situation is being exercised, it removes an entire set of options, asserting that some considerations are "off-limits." Tenure supports the continuation of programs and departments much as they currently exist, an archaic construct in a world where information doubles in less time than the typical faculty probationary period, and a large percentage of the jobs Americans will hold in the next century do not yet exist. It protects professors who refuse to consider or apply new technologies, when students are entering their classrooms fully expecting them to be part of the learning experience. It allows the tired, the worn out, and the burned out to refuse constructive opportunities for renewal and revitalization, keeping them in the classroom when everyone knows that it is a disservice to do so. It places individual faculty members in a position to thwart, subvert, and delay critical change, and occasionally serves to keep those employed in education who have clearly violated the trusts of the profession.

As the world changes, so must the academy—and tenure without periodic review stands as a major impediment. It is ironic that tenure was created to protect the voices of those who advocate radically different opinions or positions—the basis for change. Yet, it is the creature itself that now impedes its reason for being. Service-centered leadership must, if it is to serve all with a stake in the institution, implement standard reviews of tenure that *protect and encourage* academic freedom, but insure productivity and professional responsibility.

Francis Hesselbein lists, as one of the milestones to transformational change, the ability to "challenge the gospel," to decide that there are no longer sacred cows. We must, she argues, practice what she calls "planned abandonment," and in the academic world, it is time to include deep bureaucracy and tenure without periodic review as part of that herd.[7]

ORGANIZING FOR SERVICE

Organizing for service and change need not immediately be this dramatic, and can begin with something as simple as giving careful thought to how the administrative team is structured. Charles McClain, in his visionary transformation of Northeast Missouri State, began by selecting the most talented and *diverse* administrative team he could assemble. He intentionally looked for people with varied backgrounds, experiences, and attitudes, and encouraged what he referred to as a "creative tension" in his administrative meetings. One of his greatest concerns was that those working with him would think too much like he did, denying the university the richness and energy of a wide spectrum of thought and approaches. Industrialist Henry J. Kaiser is quoted as having said, "I make progress by having people around who are smarter than I am—and listening to them. And I assume that everyone is smarter about something than I am."[8]

Peter Senge, in his leadership education programs, draws upon the film *Dances With Wolves* and its reflection of the wisdom of "council" in Native American culture to help organizational leaders recognize the value of this process. Senge asks students to watch the portion of the film in which the Sioux meet in council to discuss a serious issue facing the tribe. He notes that as the issue is processed, each member has an opportunity to speak and each contribution is visibly acknowledged by the others. In one session, the tribal leader concludes by saying, "These are complex issues. It is easy to become confused. We will have to talk some more."[9]

Senge acknowledges that many managers find this approach frustrating, slow, and indecisive, but argues that new leadership for the coming century will require this kind of deliberate involvement.

THE NEW FACULTY ROLE

If for no other reason, our institutions must become less bureaucratic and more broadly representative to keep us in touch with those we serve. And the role of faculty must change to establish a greater sense of connectivity than our current cloistered existence allows. In 1996, E. Desmond Lee, a prominent St. Louis businessman, began to endow a series of faculty chairs at universities in his home community. By 2005, he, his wife, Mary Ann, and several business associates whom he encouraged to share his vision had funded 35 positions, all with a unique responsibility. Each chair has mandatory teaching responsibility and is expected to engage in scholarly work. But half of his or her responsibility must be devoted to a community partner.

Scholars in the Des Lee Collaborative Vision cover the full spectrum of disciplines, from the physical sciences, to education, to the arts. An internationally known biologist partners with the St. Louis Zoo, while a renowned botanist is assigned to the city's famous Botanical Gardens. Artists and musicians work with museums and the St. Louis symphony, and specialists in education have community responsibilities with area school districts and the state's community colleges. Professors of ethnic and cultural studies are assigned to the city's ethnic and minority communities. These unique positions assist partners with planning, grant writing, professional development workshops, and leadership education. They share the university's expertise, and bring the ideas and concerns of their partners back to the university's administration.

The Des Lee Collaborative Vision suggests what the faculty role of the future should be, and what university outreach must include to be involved in power-with relationships with their stakeholders. Whether serving in a teaching or research institution, the direction of the future should be that a number of faculty in higher education should be hired for, and assigned to, public partnership roles as critical parts of their professional responsibilities.

THE PRESIDENT AS SOCIAL ACTOR

As community partnerships grow and as external relationships become more important and complex, the president must assume the role of cheerleader, facilitator, spokesperson, and conscience. In an article reproduced in the text used by Phi Theta Kappa's national community college student leadership program, Sally Helgesen interviewed Frances Hesselbein, while Hesselbein was still serving as chief executive of the Girl Scouts. Hesselbein later became executive director of the Drucker Institute, and Helgesen credits Drucker with having called Hesselbein "perhaps the best professional manager in America." [10]

In the excerpt reprinted in the leadership text, Hesselbein explains to Sally Helgesen that she envisions the new organizational models needed to deal with the future's dynamic and responsive organizations as being circular, noting that, symbolically, circles are important. "The circle is an organic image," she says. "We speak of the *family* circle. The circle is inclusive, but it allows for flow and movement; the circle doesn't box you in. I've always conceived of management as a circular process."

To illustrate her point at the luncheon interview, Hesselbien:

> seizes a wooden pepper mill and sets it in the middle of the table. "This is me," she says, "in the middle of the organization." She moves a glass of iced tea and several packets of sugar to form a circle around the pepper mill. "And this is my management team, the first circle." Using cups and saucers, Frances Hesselbein constructs a second circle around the first. "These are the people who report to the first team. And beyond this outer circle, there's another, and another beyond that. And they're all interrelated." She picks up knives and forks and begins fashioning radials to link up the orb lines. "As the circles extend outward, there are more and more connections. So the galaxy gets more interwoven as it gets bigger."[11]
>
> For colleges and universities, these outer circles must include the greater business and civic community. The "knives and forks" must be formal links with each of these recipients of our services and investors in our success, and they must be actively exchanging information.

In addition to faculty outreach responsibilities such as those exemplified by the Des Lee Collaborative, four-year colleges and universities could draw an important lesson from community colleges where advisory groups link academic programs with the constituents they are intended to serve. Advisory committee members are selected so as to provide programs with up-to-date information about what is happening in the discipline beyond the institution, and with links to external resources that can support change when needed. Functioning at their best, these committees serve as conduits for continuous exchange between administrative representatives, faculty from both universities and community colleges, public and business leaders, and representative students. Faculty with community partnering responsibility feed information back into the organization from their areas of responsibility, and a network of participatory governance is developed that is legitimately dynamic and useful.

Those who have had experience working in China are very familiar with the importance in Chinese culture of *guanzi*, the Chinese reliance on personal relationships and trust. These relationships are, in many ways, more important than the outcomes that drive the Western sense of getting things done. For the Chinese, it is much more critical that things get done in the proper way, and that appropriate time be spent establishing and cultivating appropriate and trusting relationships. Underlying the concept of *guanzi* is the continuous Chinese Confucian emphasis on harmony, propriety, and reciprocity. While the negative side of reciprocity is "you scratch my back and I'll scratch yours," the positive side becomes one of "you look after my interests, and I'll look after yours." The president's role in the college and university of this century will include the cultivation of the positive elements of *guanzi*—to serve as principle builder and sustainer of relationships, harmony, and propriety. No college administrator who has worked with government officials, business partners, or social agencies can deny that having created and sustained a series of trusting, personal relationships furthers the cause of the institution. The president insures that appropriate time is spent on this relationship building, and becomes central to establishing those connections. He or she is present, visible, and informed, controlling pace so that there is no sense on the part of public and private partners that the institution is pushing too hard, usurping too much authority, or being insensitive to the cultural norms and expectations of partners. As the center of the circle of relationships, the president serves as beacon—keeping various participants from feeling abandoned, or from colliding, running aground, or sinking.

For the leader, a service-centered model also means more work—or at least, a significantly more involving kind of work. It means participating as peer on some occasions, as facilitator on others, and as director in still others. It means understanding the organization in a complete, holistic way so as to have a sense for where the institution is not serving as it should—where the conduits for exchanged information and influence are clogged, or where information is flowing, but is being ignored. It means getting in early and staying late, becoming infinitely patient and increasingly tough skinned. Unlike the authoritative models where the boss isn't questioned, it invites constant review and evaluation of the leader and his or her actions.

Structure, in and of itself, does not make a leader a servant-focused leader, nor does it make the college a power-with institution. It simply enables. In Greenleaf's definition of "persuasive power," persuasion means helping each individual "arrive at a feeling of rightness about a belief or action through one's own intuitive sense." Intuition is not devoid of logic in this definition, but combines it with other sources of insight available to the individual to allow the person to shape an informed decision. This process requires time, which again raises the issue of getting things done in a timely fashion.[12]

SERVANT-LEADERSHIP AND ORGANIZATIONAL EFFICIENCY

The thought of turning an important issue over to a committee is enough to make most capable leaders break into a cold sweat. Committees are notoriously slow, and are known for developing compromise decisions that may not always be the best decisions for the organization.

Shared governance cannot mean completely negotiated decision making. Sandy Baum notes, in an article written for a Lumina Foundation report on controlling college costs, that, "Successful shared governance does not require that all priorities be shared or that consensus be reached on all decisions. It does require that everyone be open to thinking in new ways and to engaging with the language and values of others."[13] At the heart of the governance issue must be the questions: Does everyone served have an opportunity to make reasonable input into organizational decisions? Is there a mechanism through which each issue can be weighed to evaluate how decisions will affect the long-term health of the institution and well-being of those it was created to serve? Does each person understand that shared governance can work only if it is "vision directed" and is accompanied by a recognition that final responsibility for the decisions must lie with those who hold principal accountability—who will have to bear the consequences of the resulting action?

Implicit in these questions is the acknowledgement that the organization must constantly be self-assessing. The last of Francis Hesselbein's eight milestones in institutional transformation is the ability to assess performance. "Self assessment," she states, "is essential to progress. Well defined action steps and a plan for measuring results are essential to planning any organizational change."[14] If higher education has a second major weakness beyond its bureaucratic resistance to change, it is its reluctance to critically self-assess. To remedy this shortcoming, a change model must be developed that imposes an independent assessment of program by program performance, and one that extends beyond the standard accreditation review.

Richland Community College in Dallas, Texas, chose to accomplish this through participation in the national Baldrige Award process, a program of state and national assessments by external teams that examines every organizational unit's program of continuous improvement. Other colleges have chosen to focus their improvement processes internally, requiring that each department annually provide a data-supported "accounting" to an independent quality management group, demonstrating what has been done to improve instruction, manage costs, develop personnel, and demonstrate effectiveness.

If we are serving as we should, students, faculty, our communities, and all who depend on the institution to produce well prepared graduates, meaningful research, and applicable scholarship have a right to know that we are doing so effectively and responsibly. They should have a clear understanding of our mission, of what that mission means in terms of educational achievement, of our measures for determining accomplishment, and of our results. If we are unable to show them those results, they should not be obligated to support us in pursuing them.

NOTES

1. Lao Tzu, *The Way of Life*, trans. Witter Bynner (New York: Putnam, 1972), 46.

2. Phil Jackson, *Sacred Hoops* (New York: Hyperion, 1996), 5.

3. Mischa Richter and Harald Bakken, Cartoon, *Chronicle of Higher Education*, 9 January 1998, B11.

4. Carole Cable, Cartoon, *Chronicle of Higher Education*, 16 January 1998, B13.

5. Francis Hesselbein, "Journey to Transformation," in *Leader to Leader* 7 (1998): 6.

6. Mischa Richter and Harald Bakken, Cartoon, *Chronicle of Higher Education*, 16 January 1998, B3.

7. Hesselbein, 6.

8. Henry J. Kaiser, http://en.thinkexist.com/quotation/i_make_progress_by_having_people_around_me_who/264169.html (accessed September 25, 2006).

9. Peter M. Senge, "Robert Greenleaf's Legacy: A New Foundation for Twenty-first Century Institutions," in *Reflections on Leadership*, ed. Larry C. Spears (New York: John Wiley & Sons, 1995), 232–233.

10. Sally Helgesen, "The Female Advantage," in *To Lead or Not To Lead* (Jackson, MS: Phi Theta Kappa, 1995), 1.35–1.36.

11. Ibid., 1.35–1.36.

12. Robert K. Greenleaf, *On Becoming a Servant Leader*, ed. Don M. Frick and L Spears (San Francisco: Jossey-Bass, 1996), 129–139.

13. Sandy Baum, "Approaching the Dilemma from Both Sides," in *Course Corrections: Experts Offer Solutions to the College Cost Crisis*, ed. Robert C. Dickeson (Indianapolis, IN: Lumina Foundation, 2005), 89.

14. Hesselbein, 7.

CHAPTER

Leading as Learning

Appreciation is largely a matter of exposure.

—Dean Farnsworth

My father was an English professor, a specialist in Elizabethan and Victorian literature. At about 14, I recall walking into the living room where my father was reading and declaring that I had started to read Shakespeare in school and didn't see anything particularly great about the guy.

My father looked up without expression and asked, "What are you reading?"

"*A Midsummer Night's Dream.*"

"How much have you read?"

"About half."

"What don't you like about it?"

"Listen to this," I declared. "'Oh, grim look night. Oh, night with hue so black.' Nobody talks like that!"

He put down his book. "Finish the play," he said. "Then you need to read *Hamlet*, then *Othello*, then *King Lear*, then *Romeo and Juliet*. Select some of the most important passages and memorize them. Recite them until you can say them as Shakespeare intended the words to be spoken, as Hamlet said to his players, 'trippingly on the tongue.' Then you will begin to understand the beauty and poetry of the language. You see," he observed, "appreciation is largely a matter of exposure."

His lesson is one that applies to all areas of life, and especially to leadership in a changing world. A leader who is not constantly learning—constantly receiving new exposures—is forever falling behind. Without continuous learning, there can be no appreciation for newly diverse communities, new technologies, new opportunities, and new areas of difficulty. During the fireside chat with Peter Vaill mentioned earlier in the book, he noted that, "Leadership is not learned; it *is* learning. In a white water world, no activity is secure. All activities are constantly in a state of transformation."[1]

The greatest complaint that I hear from many capable leaders in recent years is that they feel busier than they have ever been. They find that they need to spend more time raising money, courting legislators, and managing budgets and legal issues. For those who are trying to lead through service, the pressures to learn are compounded by the need to understand the learning challenges faced by those they serve. In this context, constant learning can provide the exposures necessary to build awareness, create new insights, find escape from what can otherwise become debilitating pressure, and seek the renewal of intellect and spirit needed to remain fresh and passionate.

LEARNING AS AWARENESS

My father's philosophy was one he constantly put into action. A few months after our Shakespeare conversation, he packed up his family of six children, ranging from 3 to 16 years of age, and moved to Iran for two years. To broaden his own exposures and those of his family, he had accepted a temporary position with the United States Information Agency in Iran to help the country develop library resources and assist with English instruction. Though he was hardly well-to-do and had to sacrifice considerably to make changes to the government provided itinerary, we traveled to the Middle East through Asia, stopping in Tokyo, Hong Kong, Bangkok, and Delhi. He chose not to live in one of the common American "compounds" while in Tehran, but rented a house north of the city where we shopped in the local markets, had our hair cut by Persian barbers rather than at the American Club, and tried to immerse ourselves in Iranian culture.

During the family's return to the United States two years later, he bought a Volkswagen bus, a tent, and camping gear in Germany, and we drove south, starting in Italy and making our way north through the campgrounds of Europe. He dragged us, tired and road weary, into the open-air amphitheater at the Baths at Caricalla to see *Aida* performed with live camels and elephants on the old Roman stage. In the evenings, he pulled out his guitar, invited the multinational campers in the tents around us to gather around the Coleman stove, and sang American folk songs. "On Springfield Mountain" turned out to be a favorite, since the chorus, "To rudi ney, to rudi new" made sense to no one and therefore served as a universal language.

The message was always the same. Appreciation is a matter of exposure—positive exposure—and the same is true with leadership. A faculty colleague I particularly admire, a scientist and mathematician named Art Boyt, had a remarkably similar experience as a young man. His father, a community college art instructor, took advantage of a job change when Art was 16 to spend seven months traveling with his family through Europe. The seven of them lived in a decrepit motor home, shopped in the local markets for groceries, and made a point of being everywhere in the off-season to make the trip affordable. One of Art's most vivid memories is of a frosty morning lying beneath the van, heating the butane tank with a candle to generate enough vapor for the morning coffee. From this vantage point, he watched a growing pack of Dutch children whoosh by on bikes on their way to school, with clouds of frozen breath trailing behind like engine exhaust. As they passed each home, new riders joined the group, and Art recalls feeling the free exhilaration of the riders, contrasting it to the monotonous hours in bumpy school buses he had experienced on dusty Iowa back roads.

"I believe in Eureka moments," Art explained, when relating the moment, "times when new experiences create new directions in one's life. I think they come most often when you are exposed to things which occur outside of the routine of normal daily life."[2]

Those moments have profoundly influenced Art and his thinking. He was a member of the group who developed the first solar powered vehicle to cross the United States in 1984, and he and his father designed the solar-powered vehicle, STAR II, that won the engineering design award in General Motors's first trans-America Sunrayce. He credits his own innovative abilities and leadership awareness to these experiences, and to the constant emphasis in his early life on learning.

If vision is a principal role of leadership, how can the leader *envision* if there is not constant learning? How can he or she project and anticipate, determine how diverse members of the organizational community will respond? Even as a full-time learner, no leader can expect to keep abreast of everything—even those events and developments that are essential to good organizational management. Learning must become *every* employee's responsibility, part of the organizational fabric, and the institution must structure ways in which that learning can be shared internally and with the broader community through travel-study opportunities, brown bag lunches, informal reading groups, and other strategies designed to keep people intellectually engaged.

LEARNING AS INSIGHT

The difference between learning as awareness and learning as insight might appear largely semantic, but I believe there is a subtle and important distinction. By *awareness*, I am referring to an increase in general knowledge about, or experience with, something new. *Insight* extends that awareness by providing new ways of seeing and understanding based upon this knowledge and experience.

Some years ago, I joined 15 other educators as part of a Fulbright-Hays summer fellowship to Pakistan to study Shariah, Islamic Law, as it was being applied to the country's secular legal code. During the six weeks, we met with prominent social, governmental, religious, and business leaders in five regions of this diverse nation. The entire experience was an "awareness" builder, from the moment we arrived in Islamabad until we left Karachi. Each day also created new insights, and one in particular demonstrated a lesson I have often seen repeated.

Three particularly memorable days were spent in the village of Kalam in the Swat Valley, a remote region of the Northwest Frontier province. Kalam nestles beside the Swat River at the end of a precarious mountain road at about the 7,000-foot level in the foothills of the Himalayas. It had remained relatively untouched, with most foreigners who visited the northern provinces choosing the more accessible villages along the Karakoram Highway or venturing farther west toward Gujarat.

Electricity had not yet reached Kalam—at least not by power line—but our small guesthouse did have a generator, which operated a few hours each evening. During these precious hours, a cluster of villagers gathered around a television set in the hostel's dining area to watch programming beamed via satellite from Hong Kong. One of those hours was filled with reruns of the American soap opera, *Santa Barbara.*

At breakfast early one morning, I attempted a conversation with one of the proprietor's sons, an assertive boy in his early teens with a halting command of English learned in the village school. After exchanging a few phrases from his memorized dialogues, he paused for a moment, and then asked, "You are American?"

"Yes," I said.

"Do you know Kelly and Laken?"

"Kelly and Laken?" I asked.

"Yes ... from Santa Barbara."

As the conversation progressed, I realized that, to this young teenager from northern Pakistan, America was simply a replication of his Upper Swat Valley home—a cluster of villages where families had lived for generations and everyone knew everyone else. It was also apparent that he believed television simply to be an open window on the real life, day-to-day activities in the village of Santa Barbara. Since I was American, it must be near where I lived, and I must know Kelly and Laken.

Though there was a touching lesson in his provincialism, the boy's questions taught me a great deal more about technology and its uses. Marvelous electronic capabilities in and of themselves do not extend our capacities to see, do, or understand, as long as we apply them within the same limited contexts to which we have applied other ways of knowing. Television, for this boy, was simply a visit to another village. Unless those using technology can envision new contexts and can explore them in previously unimagined ways, these new tools offer only greater efficiency, not greater understanding. It is an insight I have been able to apply as I have struggled with my own use of technology and with encouraging others to find creative ways to use it.

I am not at all certain where insight comes from—what happens in our heads to connect previously unconnected bits of information in creative new ways. But I am convinced that it happens more often when we are active and diverse learners. One of the most useful observations I have come across about learning

was actually written as advice to art students by a practitioner interested in recommending those experiences that might be useful in developing insight. In *The
Shape of Content*, artist/writer Ben Shahn wrote:

> Attend a university if you possibly can. There is no content of knowledge
> that is not pertinent to the work you will want to do. But before you attend a
> university, work at something for a while. Do anything. Get a job in a potato
> field; or work as a grease monkey in an auto repair shop. But if you do work in
> a field, do not fail to observe the look and feel of earth and of all things you
> handle—yes, even potatoes. Or, in the auto shop, the smell of oil and grease
> and burning rubber.... Listen well to all conversations and be instructed by
> them and take all seriousness seriously. Never look down on anything or
> anyone as not worthy of notice. In college or out of college, read. And form
> opinions! Read Sophocles and Euripides and Dante and Proust.... Read the
> Bible; read Hume; read Pogo.... Know all that you can, both curricular and
> non-curricular—mathematics and physics and economics, logic and particu-
> larly history. Know at least two languages besides your own.... Talk and talk
> and sit at cafes, and listen to everything, to Brahms, to Brubeck, to the Italian
> hour on the radio. Listen to preachers in small town churches and in big city
> churches. Listen to politicians in New England town meetings and to rabble-
> rousers in Alabama.... And remember that you are trying to learn to think
> what you want to think ... never be afraid to undertake any kind of art at all,
> however exalted or however common, but do it with distinction.[3]

Shahn realized that insight, in art as in life, is the product of pulling together
widely differing experiences and recognizing that they are connected in uniquely
interesting and useful ways. This observation takes me back to a criticism expressed
as a generalization in the first chapter—that we are, as educators, isolated and
insulated from much of the world. We are inclined to mistake being educated for
being informed, even when our own professional specialties are narrowly focused.
We are prone to say, "I am constantly learning. I review five journals a week, read
three new monographs in my discipline each month, and listen to NPR." Yet
learning for insight demands that we step outside of the general confines of our
naturally occurring experiences. It requires that we force new learning opportunities where they would not occur without conscious intervention.

Jim Tatum, the trustee mentioned earlier who initially directed my attention to
Greenleaf and his writing, is a case study in learning to gain insight. He is a West
Point graduate who aspired to military leadership in his early life, and possesses
all of the characteristics. He is a tall, striking man with a brilliant mind and an
engaging personality.

During the Korean conflict, he was seriously wounded leading a group of men
in combat, the first of a number of life-changing epiphanies for Jim. The wounds
ended his military career, and the experience of struggling with dying soldiers who
were under his charge initiated a search for greater purpose and meaning. He is a
man who has determined that "search" is an action verb—one that requires a willingness to risk and to initiate. He is a voracious reader of material in almost every

discipline, and when he comes across an idea that intrigues him, he picks up the phone and calls the person who introduced him to it. It was this boldness which first connected Jim with Robert Greenleaf, a man with whom he became good friends. He has contacted Rushworth Kidder about rediscovering values in society, Parker Palmer about returning spirit to the workplace, and Sister Joel Read about Alverno College's success at incorporating both of these efforts into college life. He is as likely to call if he strongly disagrees as agrees, believing that, in learning why someone feels so adamantly opposed to a view which he holds, he will come to better understand his own position. Gaining insight, he will be quick to tell you, is an active, engaging process. Unless each of us forces learning beyond our immediate circumstance and our natural circle of interests, new insights rarely come.

LEARNING AS ESCAPE

Warren Bennis opens his book on *Why Leaders Can't Lead* by recounting the death of an acting college president who, after a particularly grueling week, drove his automobile around a bend into the front of a logging truck, killing him instantly. The death was ruled accidental, though many on campus wondered. The president had been under tremendous pressure, had recently suffered a major professional disappointment when passed over for the permanent position, and the stress and depression had been evident to many at the college.[4]

Every college leader has had one of those weeks and has said to him- or herself, "Why do I do this? There must be *something* I could do that wouldn't subject me to this kind of pressure." Yet most of us are also willing to admit that leading in the academic world is as satisfying as anything we can imagine. We love what we do, and in some ways, the challenges and pressures are part of what makes the job exciting and continually interesting. But pressure can become debilitating, and the job of serving and healing becomes increasingly difficult if the leader is unable to heal personally. Learning can become a great healer and a great avenue for escape from the mental and physical pressures of leadership.

In an article in the *Chronicle* some years ago, Courtney Leatherman described the "escape mechanisms" developed by a number of the nation's educational chief executive officers (CEOs) to relieve the incessant pressures of the job. Some presidents, she noted, described the job as "7X24—seven days a week, 24 hours a day. They work a lot and they sleep a little."[5] The issue received considerable national attention in 1982 when president Jay Carsey simply disappeared from his job at Charles County Community College, only to surface seven years later in another position in education. In his book, *Exit the Rainmaker*, Carsey described the relentless demands that led to his disappearance.

Concern over the problems of pressure in the college presidency peaked in 1994, when Harvard president Neil Rudenstine took a leave of absence to recover from exhaustion, and many began to ask if the job was even manageable. In her article, Leatherman identified the mechanisms a number of CEOs have adopted to release the tensions of the workplace.[6]

One president practiced magic and performed for friends and at community events. "A high-quality magician has an incredible understanding of the human mind," he noted in the article.

Another scheduled a 6:00 A.M. workout with a weight trainer three days a week, and periodically checked into a Roman Catholic retreat house where she spent a week in quiet study and meditation. "When I became president," she observed, "I realized what my life was often missing was opportunity for reflection, so I began to seek that, and finally realized that the best way to find it was to go to a place that did that full time."[7]

A third practiced tai chi, the ancient oriental meditative art of controlled movement and breathing, noting that the daily routine gave them "a certain degree of calmness and equilibrium."[8]

It is not coincidental that, in each of these cases, the escape combined physical and intellectual diversion. Both the mind and body need release from the stresses and intense focus of college administration, and learning to do or to think something completely removed from that routine can be the perfect form of escape.

LEARNING AS RENEWAL

All academic leaders began their professional lives as something else, often as professors in a discipline chosen because of a deep and lasting interest in the field. It may have been a profound love of literature, a fascination with the intricacies and predictability of the laws of physics, or a desire to thoroughly understand the world's financial markets that initially drew them into academic life. Once in administrative positions, time constraints and irregular schedules often make it difficult to continue to pursue these interests, and the result can be a loss of intellectual vigor. The enjoyment, the passion that was associated with work in the specific discipline disappears when the intellectual climate changes and the leader becomes immersed day after day in the mundane issues that fill typical administrative calendars. Even the challenging issues are of a different nature, and do not excite the mind in the same way those initial academic passions did. For some, the loss is too great and most of us know someone who has chosen to return to teaching or research. Even those who enjoy the stimulation of administrative challenges find that they are not a complete substitute for the intellectual satisfactions that come from teaching or academic study.

A close colleague and 17-year veteran of the college presidency has an academic background in music and law. He found the intellectual renewal he needed through active volunteer leadership in the state Arts Council, where he served for many years as chair, and continues to be involved in program planning. While president, he kept his fingers in the classroom by annually teaching a leadership course for emerging community leaders, using a curriculum based upon classic studies in leadership drawn from great literature and film.

Service is giving, and without some mechanism for renewal, a serving leader can easily give away more energy than can be spared. To serve well, one must first serve oneself and find those activities that keep the body active and alert, and the soul renewed.

NOTES

1. Peter Vaill, "A Fireside Chat with Peter Vaill," *Peter Vaill Presentation* (Robert K. Greenleaf Center for Servant-Leadership, 1996), audio cassette recording.

2. Art Boyt, personal conversation, 12 September 1995.

3. Ben Shahn, *The Shape of Content* (Cambridge, MA: Harvard University Press, 1972), 113–114.

4. Warren Bennis, *Why Leaders Can't Lead* (San Francisco: Jossey-Bass, 1989), 3–5.

5. Courtney Leatherman, "How Some Presidents Keep Their Cool Amid Campus Crises and 60-Hour Weeks," *Chronicle of Higher Education*, 6 February 1998, A36.

6. Ibid.

7. Ibid.

8. Ibid.

CHAPTER

Barriers to Leadership as Service

There is no necessary connection between the desire to lead and the
ability to lead, and even less the ability to lead somewhere that will be
to the advantage to the led.

—Bergen Evens

I f the key element to creating a service-centered organization is an institutional
vision that sees all stakeholders growing as fully and positively as possible, it
stands to reason that elements that impede the creation of common vision and
limit personal growth are the enemies of service-centered leadership. The best
intentioned and most deeply committed president can be rendered impotent by
any number of opposing interests that are addressed in this chapter, with a brief
return at the end to a discussion of personal presidential actions that can also serve
as barriers to effective leadership.

THE BOARD AS BARRIER

At least in the public sector, the most critical aid or barrier to effective institutional governance is the college governing board. In a greatly simplified sense,
board members fall into three categories: self-centered, constituency-centered,
and institution-centered. The self-centered seek appointment or election to further personal agendas or ambitions—to get rid of someone, protect a favorite
program, initiate a political career, attempt to manipulate programs and policies
for personal gain or, in cases in which trustees are paid, to supplement income.
These are the disgruntled employees who leave the institution then seek positions

on the board to reap havoc on the administration or the unfortunate who offended them. They are the football trustees who would sacrifice the entire humanities department for an all-American running back. They are political hacks who see a spot on the regional college board as a jumping-off point for the state legislature, or the perennial part-time student who suddenly realizes that, by mobilizing quiet student support during a low turnout election, he can become a trustee and affect college policy. At least initially, these trustees stand in the way of service-centered leadership. Unless they are able to subordinate their personal agendas to a larger institutional vision, they will constantly be impeding, misdirecting, and subverting the college.

The constituency-centered trustee shares many of the same motives, but pursues them on behalf of a special interest group. When this action is directed toward seeking what is best for the institution as a whole, few problem arise. When this is not the case, these board members can be just as damaging to effective administration. In their minds, they represent the faculty, labor, the " antitax" coalition, the booster club, or some other group with a specific agenda. They see their role as protecting and furthering the interests of that particular constituency, with little regard for the effects of their input and decisions on other areas of institutional life and health. If appointed, some view the appointment as a mandate to further the fiscal responsibility agenda of the state administration, to support advancement of a particular ethnic group, or to enact specific programmatic change. These causes, in and of themselves, are not necessarily undesirable, but become so when they slip blinders over the eyes of the board member and limit a view of the broader institutional picture.

Though often called *curators*, *governors*, or *regents*, all are "trustees," and the designation is not accidental. It is descriptive of the responsibilities accompanying the office, those of holding *in trust* the present and future of the college or university and its role in serving *all* stakeholders. Most boards swear to an oath of office; an oath that they will honor that trust. To continue to focus solely on personal or limited constituency issues is a violation of trust and trusteeship, and it is the responsibility of the board chair and each of the board's members to regularly reeducate themselves to that reality.

Sister to this basic principle of board member as *trustee* is the understanding that boards are committees of the whole; that no single person is "the board." Acting alone, trustees have no legitimate authority, and unless authorized by the committee of the whole to do so, no one speaks for the board but the board chair when expressing mutually agreed upon positions. To give opinions about institutional issues outside of the context of the board as a whole is a violation of trusteeship, and subordinates service to self. Boards can do much to support the institution by abiding by the same rule of consensus described earlier, the rule that decisions will be processed until each member can either be supportive or agree sufficiently so as not to oppose. If unable to reach this consensus, members should reexamine their positions to determine if a sense of institutional benefit is standing in the way of agreement, or if personal or constituent interests are interfering.

In recent years, several developments in trusteeship have exacerbated these problems and their influences on institutional effectiveness. Trusteeship has, at least in the public sector, traditionally been an unpaid, voluntary opportunity to serve. In some states, most notably California, it is evolving into a paid political position, and a reasonably lucrative one. When we lose voluntary trusteeship, we begin to lose an attitude and commitment at the policy making level that is key to the development of servant-led institutions. In a moving speech to the 1980 Volunteer Leaders Conference of United Way of America, Notre Dame's president emeritus, Theodore Hesburgh, called volunteerism "the heart of what has made America great and unique."[1] He issued a warning that we were in the process of losing much of the value that has come to America through volunteerism, turning those responsibilities over to government. Though public higher education certainly *is* government in many ways, one of its unique strengths has been the voluntary leadership provided by lay governing boards. They bring to education the commitment and spirit noted by de Tocqueville, and quoted by Hesburgh in his address:

> Although private interest directs the greater part of human action in the United States as well as elsewhere, it does not regulate them all. I must say that I have often seen Americans make great and real sacrifices to the public welfare; and I have noticed a hundred instances in which they hardly ever failed to lend faithful support to one another. The free institutions which the inhabitants of the United States possess, and the political rights of which they make so much use, remind every citizen, and in a thousand ways, that he lives in a society. They every instant impress upon his mind the notion that it is the duty as well as the interest of men to make themselves useful to their fellow creatures; and as he sees no particular ground of animosity to them, since he is never either their master or their slave, his heart readily leans to the side of kindness. Men attend to the interests of the public, first by necessity, afterward by choice; what was intentional becomes an instinct, and by dint of working for the good of one's fellow citizens, the habit and the taste for serving them are at length acquired.[2]

To lose the volunteer nature of the trustee role would be a blow both to education as public servant and to the development of service-centered leadership. Trusteeship that may initially have been created as a volunteer service by necessity, and has evolved into one by choice, must continue to gain its rewards from the opportunities to serve—otherwise service gives way to personal gain and greed.

It might be argued that members of the boards of independent colleges, many of whom are selected based upon their abilities to give or get money, can be held to a different standard of commitment and service. Not if they serve as the policymaking body for the institution. If they are purely fundraisers, put them on foundation boards. If they are shaping policy that determines the services provided to students, faculty, and community, they too should be servants first. There are, fortunately, many individuals who are capable of and willing to do both.

PERSONNEL BARRIERS

The challenges that impede service-centered leadership within the organization are also frequently people issues. We have already discussed the problems created by those who do not share institutional vision—or who have a different understanding of that vision. If Follett's process for creative conflict resolution is working and members are able to air those differences honestly, issues related to interpretation and emphasis can generally be worked out. When there is basic disagreement about the mission, the problem becomes more serious and the solution may require that a member—president or employee—find employment elsewhere. The alternative is an employee who continues to be uncomfortable with the vision being pursued and becomes isolated or marginalized in an attempt to minimize contamination.

More destructive, however, are those who cannot trust. As the old Dean Witter commercial said, "We are not born with an instinct to trust," and some, for any number of reasons, seem unable to share trust and place it in others. How does a leader work with those who choose not to trust? By inviting them to work within the system anyway, by freely allowing them to express their suspicions, and by never providing justification for their concerns.

Occasionally groups within the organization will demonstrate this same suspicion, lack of trust, or unreasonable expectation. Personnel associations, unions, and even departments may feel pressure or obligation to represent a position or protect an individual when it is clearly not in the best interest of the collective whole to do so. In some cases, representatives of these groups argue that their function is to defend the interests of members of that group, right or wrong, and when this is the spirit, it becomes very difficult to engender institution-wide trust.

An article covering a strike by faculty at a Philadelphia college who were demanding salary increases and an early retirement plan illustrates the problem. A college spokeswoman explained that the institution was attempting to recover from an eight million dollar deficit and could not meet union demands and restore institutional health at the same time, but faculty appeared unmoved by the institution's plight.[3] The message seemed to be, "We don't really care about the college as a whole, or its future. We only care about ourselves." It may very well be that the deficit resulted from poor administration, but the solution certainly was not to compound the college's financial woes. If power-with is exercised as it should be, everyone examines the budget annually, contributes to decisions, shares responsibility for deficits and surpluses, and understands what needs to be done to keep the institution healthy. Complete disclosure by the administration, when not prohibited by law or issues of confidentiality, is essential if this is to happen, and can do much to soften the unreasonable requests by special interest groups by creating an assurance that, in every case, the best interests of all will be taken into account. Some of the seriously adversarial situations that exist in the country between administrations and powerful employee unions and associations may seem beyond repair. But if trust, full disclosure, and a legitimate effort to share power are exercised over time, these situations can be salvaged.

Recognition that the most troublesome barriers to effective leadership are often people issues highlights the critical role that employee selection plays in establishing institutional climate and success. Position announcements should indicate that the college is seeking individuals who prefer to work in an environment of shared decision making and responsibility. Applications should ask for evidence that the person can work effectively with integrated teams. Reference calls should focus as much on demonstration of caring, trust, and willingness to work collaboratively as on other areas of job performance and scholarship. And the interview must allow those involved in the selection process to judge the ability to cooperate, adjust to change, and discuss honestly and without defensiveness. No academic credential should be allowed to compensate for failure to be a caring human being.

A *Chronicle* position announcement by a college looking for a new CEO (chief executive officer) illustrated how early expressions of vision and enduring institutional values can shape the kind of applicant who chooses to apply. In the ad, the college announced:

- We embrace teaching and learning as our central purpose.
- We make every effort to help learners achieve success.
- We respect differences in people and ideas.
- We plan and work together with respect, trust, and honesty within the college and with the communities we serve.
- We seek the best possible ways to conduct our work.

The message seems clear: autocrats and those not committed to service need not apply. *Every* position ad should include some statement of expectation that goes beyond basic academic and experiential qualifications, and those expectations should be reinforced throughout the entire selection process. There will, of course, be those outstanding scholars who have very little interest in serving students, their colleagues, or the community with anything other than the product of their scholarly work. If the university can afford this kind of limited contribution and wants it to enhance some sense of so-called reputation, find the person an office or laboratory somewhere and let the scholar work. But be prepared to explain how the contribution adds in significant ways to pursuit of the vision.

INTERORGANIZATIONAL BARRIERS

Several critical barriers to service-centered leadership and to institutional transformation are external to the organization, making them even more difficult to address than the personnel challenges just reviewed. Virtually every large network of related organizations establishes some system of common standards, some quality control mechanism to ensure that products and services exchanged within the network complement and support each other. In higher education, that system is accreditation, the process by which institutions and programs are evaluated and "certified" as meeting standards that can be accepted by others as guaranteeing quality.

Though essential to maintaining the integrity of our system of higher education, accreditation in its various forms also serves as one of the major impediments to positive institutional improvement. Unless a college or university, by reason of reputation, *is* the standard, the institution takes great risk if it determines that it could better serve students by radically altering its curriculum. Although the major accrediting bodies in the United States base their reviews on how successfully institutions are meeting the goals of their expressed missions, there is also an expectation that the mechanisms for accomplishing the mission will generally be in line with the rest of the education community and with established tradition. Interinstitutional pressures also serve to have a controlling and moderating effect on unilateral change—an effect that inhibits innovation and can interfere with an institution's ability to better serve.

A state system of higher education recently experienced major trauma when the flagship university decided to significantly revamp its teacher education curriculum, transitioning from a course-based model to a competency-based model. An associate dean in the College of Education innocently sent a letter to all of the other colleges and universities in the state announcing that, beginning with the next academic year, students would no longer be able to transfer teacher education courses into the university's program, but would need to complete all of that work within the newly revised curriculum.

Response from the rest of higher education in the state, particularly the community college sector, was swift, politically charged, and effective. These institutions made it clear that the change violated the state's articulation agreements, disadvantaged students whose welfare *they* were charged with representing, and really could not be competency based if only one set of courses was recognized as building the competencies. The threat of further codifying articulation through legislative action brought the university to its knees and thwarted what might otherwise have been a very positive development for teacher education in the state.

Accreditation, articulation, and other quality control mechanisms are essential within the profession, but we must find ways to extend the model of organizational integration and collaboration to *systems* as well as to single institutions, allowing parts of the larger system to experiment, transform, and pursue a broader vision without being reigned in at the first indication of innovation. Councils of presidents using the primus inter pares model and exercising principles of the Law of the Situation and power-with must establish mechanisms through which institutions can change and evolve without creating new difficulties for students, and without destroying the integrity of the greater whole.

The higher education community must also develop methods for ensuring that those bodies that license and accredit institutions are also growing and evolving.

When the Higher Learning Commission of the North Central Association initially introduced its AQIP (Academic Quality Improvement Program) approach to accreditation, it demonstrated a number of innovative elements that showed promise of embracing change. The first set of standards mirrored the national quality award standards used by the Baldrige award process, and colleges were told that if their states had quality award programs, its assessment criteria and evaluative process could be used as the accreditation review. But even before the first set of participating colleges could complete the review process, the guidelines were forced back toward the traditional model. Rather than using evaluation teams from the state quality award programs, AQIP was forced to create its own teams of evaluators. The Baldrige criteria were modified so that colleges interested in pursuing state and national quality awards could not use the same set of standards, but had to manage two parallel assessment systems. What showed promise as an interesting and potentially groundbreaking innovation in quality assurance was traditionalized before it could be thoroughly tested.

My crystal ball tells me that the Western Governors' University model foreshadows the answer to several of these dilemmas: a gradual transition away from credit hours as the common currency for higher education, moving toward competency-based education. When this transition is complete, accrediting bodies will simply come to review how an institution's competency standards compare with those of the rest of the profession and to evaluate how successfully students are achieving the established standards. It will be an assessment of how effectively we have assisted students in becoming informed, contributing citizens rather than an evaluation of the steps we took to get them there.

THE BARRIERS OF PERKS

Returning now to the office of the presidency and potential personal barriers, Geoffrey Ashe recounts in his biography of the life of Mohandas Gandhi that, once the Indian leader had determined to seek home rule for India, "Gandhi's first positive move was in the matter of clothing." Upon returning to India from South Africa, where Gandhi's campaign for the rights of Indian citizens had established him as a national hero in his home country, Ashe states that the Mahatma "had taken to wearing a *dhoti*—an ample kind of loincloth—instead of trousers ... and tried to blend into the crowd of the poor. Though he always denied that he chose his clothes for public-relations purposes, their value from that point of view was incontestable."[4]

Gandhi's choice of dress is not an indication that every servant leader should dress as do those who are served. It simply illustrates that service requires approachability rather than separation, and that the service-centered leader must forever be conscious of those accouterments of office that create distance rather than a sense of access and trust. In most cases, these symbols are not related to dress at all, but are special perks, benefits, or behaviors that, by their nature, separate the leader from those being led.

There are, of course, special benefits that must be available to the president to do the job effectively: a travel budget and transportation allowance, an entertainment account, comfortable office, and so forth. But many leaders measure their success by pushing the limits of these benefits and by collecting other baubles that are no more than displays of power-over. At the most basic end of the bauble spectrum are free meals from college food service, coming into work late when other responsibilities have not required the president to be elsewhere, and other selective but unnecessary favors to the office. Others in the organization can't help but ask, "Why does the person best able to pay his or her own way (other than perhaps the football coach and medical school faculty) get free cafeteria meals?" The servant-leader should purchase personal tickets to plays, concerts, sporting events, and lecture series at rates asked of other members of the college employee community. When provided as perks, the message is, "I am a more important member of this community than you are," not, "I am here to help you do your job as successfully as possible."

Granted, the president and other ranking officials do need to be at functions, need to be visible, and need to host guests—creating significant expense over the course of the year. But those are the reasons for entertainment allowances and part of the reason for larger salaries. Plus, most presidents expect other members of the academic community to show support for college functions, with or without the perks. If it is an official expectation, costs to the CEO should be no less than to all those expected to attend. All should be held to the same standard.

One college president who consciously tries to exemplify the servant-leader philosophy is assigned an automobile from the college fleet and refuses to drive the newest vehicle, believing that it should be available for general college use. Her campus has no special parking for administrators, though it does for faculty. The president's comment is, "If I'm not here early enough to get a close space, I deserve to walk." This same president is as likely to answer the phone in her office as is her secretary, and believes that if her secretary is in the middle of something and she is free, she should pick up the phone. She admits that some of this is for appearance, believing that the appearance creates an attitude of primus inter pares among those with whom she works.

When I first came to the college presidency, I sat down with my new assistant and discussed office protocol. When asked what she would like in a working relationship, she said, "Please don't ask me to get you coffee, and don't ask me to buy presents for your wife. Otherwise I'll do everything I can to help you be successful." Although she told me years later that the "coffee comment was partly in jest," it was her way of saying, "When you ask me to do menial or personal things, you are showing that you don't respect me as a professional person." Please, she was saying, ask me to serve, but not to be a servant.

The president who insisted on putting the newest college vehicle into the fleet illustrates that there are actually only two kinds of outward symbols of leadership—those that unnecessarily remind others of position and authority, and those that consciously demonstrate partnership, fairness, consideration and service. The servant-leader chooses to have an attractive, comfortable and accommodating office, but not a lavish one, and asks to be treated in other areas of campus life as he or she would like others to be treated on campus. Decorum and authority do not have to be sacrificed to approachability.

Three circumstances regularly surface when examining why presidents fail: fiscal irresponsibility, unethical behavior, and failing to focus enough attention on
campus issues. There are, of course, system administrators without direct campus
responsibility for whom campus contact might appear to be less an issue. But having been part of a three-campus system at one time, I know how easily a "we-they"
attitude develops if system-wide officials are never seen on the campuses.

A good friend and colleague, a leader of one of the largest public institutions
in the nation, found himself at odds with his campus community, board, and
constituents due, in part, to his pursuit of a national office and inattention to
campus needs. This, coupled with a perception in the community of personal
and institutional extravagance, forced a resignation. The symbols of self had too
drastically overshadowed the symbols of service.

In the corporate world, exorbitant salaries among CEOs have become symbolic of misdirected leadership, reinforcing a view that personal and corporate
gain, rather than contributing to public betterment, are the be-all and end-all of
business activity. Each year, the *Chronicle of Higher Education* runs the results of
surveys of educational salaries, and annually we see salaries that are 10 to 20 times
the average paid to the institutions teaching and research professionals. A board
member at one of the private institutions with a million dollar CEO justified the
expense by pointing out that the president was a highly successful fundraiser and
had attracted additional millions to the college. True as this may be, the function
of the college is not raising money or creating profit, but extending opportunity.
When it comes right down to it, who is more valuable to the college? Is it the
fundraiser, or the three or four key professors whose dedicated work with students
over the years has fostered the loyal alumni following that produces that sizable
endowment? A leader committed to the vision of the "university as builder of
people and ideas" should expect reasonable compensation, but should also wish
to invest every other possible resource in achieving that vision.

Lest this be mistaken as some kind of egalitarian diatribe, I firmly believe that
entrepreneurs in the business world should be entitled to the riches generated by
their ideas, risk taking, and management skill—though I would encourage them to
think seriously about where lasting value lies and where they might be able to do a
greater good. But for those in the service sector, those who have chosen "serving"
as their professions, service must come before personal wealth, and that means
directing money that might go to exorbitant salaries back into the organization.

THE BARRIERS WITHIN

Perhaps the most insidious barriers to leadership as service lie within the heart
and mind of the leader—in the measure of his or her own commitment, courage,
and determination. These are the barriers described so eloquently by Robert Kennedy in a 1966 address at the University of Capetown to an audience faced with
one of history's most daunting challenges to change, transform, and serve. Kennedy identified four dangers that strew the path of leadership for those who accept

the challenge of championing institutional transformation. They are particularly apropos to one who chooses the road of service. I list them here in edited form as he spoke them, because I could not state them better:

> First, is the danger of futility; the belief that there is nothing one man or one woman can do against the enormous array of the world's ills—against misery and ignorance, injustice and violence. Yet many of the world's great movements, of thought and action, have flowed from the thought of a single man. A young monk began the Protestant reformation, a young general extended an empire from Macedonia to the borders of the earth, a young woman reclaimed the territory of France…. It is from numberless diverse acts of courage and belief that human history is shaped….
>
> The second danger is that of expediency; of those who say that hopes and beliefs must bend before immediate necessity…. [But] idealism, high aspirations and deep conviction are not incompatible with the most practical and efficient of programs; there is no basic inconsistency between ideals and realistic possibilities….
>
> A third danger is timidity…. Moral courage is a rarer commodity than bravery in battle or great intelligence. Yet it is the one essential, vital quality for those who seek to change a world which yields most painfully to change….
>
> For the fortunate among us, the fourth danger is comfort; the temptation to allow the easy and familiar paths of personal ambition and financial success so grandly spread before those who have the privilege of education…. There is a Chinese curse that says, "May you live in interesting times." Like it or not, we live in interesting times. They are times of danger and uncertainty; but they are also more open to the creative energy of men than any other time in history. And everyone here will ultimately be judged—will ultimately judge himself—on the effort which he has contributed to building a new world society and the extent to which his ideals and goals have shaped that effort.[5]

We are indeed living in dangerous times, made more so by the intangible nature of the crises we face. They are intangible to a large degree because they are not challenges of resources, but of resourcefulness; not of capacity, but of capability. They lie largely within, and call for bold new leaders whose personal courage and willingness to persevere are equal to those dangers.

NOTES

1. Theodore Hesburgh, "Reflections on Voluntarism in America," vol. XLVI no. 16, of *Vital Speeches of the Day* (Phoenix, AZ: McMurry, 1980), 485.

2. Hesburgh, citing Alexis de Tocqueville, *Democracy in America*, vol. 2 (New York: Vintage Books), 114.

3. "Community College Instructors Demand Higher Wages and Better Benefits," *Chronicle of Higher Education*, 20 March 1998, A10.

4. Geoffrey Ashe, *Gandhi* (New York: Stein and Day, 1968), 147–148.

5. Robert F. Kennedy, "Day of Affirmation," *Historical Resources*, John F. Kennedy Presidential Library and Museum Archives, 6 June 1966, http://www.jfklibrary.org/Historical+Resources/Archives/Reference+Desk/Speeches/RFK/Day+of+Affirmation+Address+News+Release.htm (accessed June 15, 2006).

CHAPTER 14

Leadership for a New Century

The supreme value is not the future but the present. The future is a deceitful time that always says, 'Not yet,' and thus denies us.

—Octavio Paz

The future enters into us, in order to transform itself in us, long before it happens.

—Rainer Maria Rilke

Several decades ago, I read with some skepticism a prediction by Alvin Toffler in his popular look at the future, *The Third Wave*, in which he asserted that: "Humanity faces a quantum leap forward. It faces the deepest social upheaval and creative restructuring of all time. Without clearly realizing it, we are engaged in building a remarkable new civilization from the ground up."[1] I wrote the quote down and have used it since in presentations, but still have been surprised by its accuracy. I suspect even Toffler did not anticipate the convergence of events, inventions, and attitudes that promise to make the twenty-first century remarkably different from the one from which he wrote.

In interrelated ways—some closely, some more loosely—five remarkable transformations have come together at this moment in history. Graham Greene, speaking of childhood, once observed that there is always one moment when the door opens and lets the future in. As children in a new world of phenomenal technological change, that moment for us appears to be now. To extend Toffler's imagery, the developments in technology have surged over us like some great tidal wave, sweeping away old ways of working, of relating to each other, and of spending our leisure time. One manifestation of this tide has been the explosion in information, and in our access to it. These two transformations—in information, and in technology in general—are often discussed as being synonymous, but have unique and critical differences that require separate examination.

A third transformation has been geopolitical. In less time than most of us dreamed possible, we have witnessed a "self-determination" revolution that divided the former Soviet Union into independent republics, is fracturing smaller nations into ethnic and religious divisions seeking greater autonomy, and threatens despotic rule in its last bastions around the globe. A "socialist free market" economy is driving development in China and Vietnam at a pace that will certainly place China as the dominant economy by the end of this century, and India will follow closely.

The fourth transformation has been the inevitable consequence of explosive population growth and the accompanying increases in human consumption. We have tapped the earth's resources to the point that, whether or not one accepts the views that we have a very narrow window of opportunity to reverse global warming trends and find alternative sources of energy, we all recognize that dramatic changes must occur in the way we manage the planet's resources. With rapidly developing standards of living in what we once considered parts of the third world, we simply cannot consume at our present rate without transforming the way we produce food, energy, and consumable materials.

In the very roots of our society, a fifth transformation is occurring. The twenty-first century will be the first in the history of the human species into which we entered, at least in Western society, with commitment to gender and racial equality. We have hardly achieved that goal, but it is now legally drawn, publicly stated, and vigorously pursued—conditions that have never existed before. Yet at the same time, we have made little progress in closing the divide between the haves, and have-nots, but have empowered the have-nots to demand greater economic and social equity. Of the five mentioned, this transformation may be the least predictable, and potentially the most consequential.

Edmund Burke, in a letter to a member of the British National Assembly written as the eighteenth century was drawing to a close, cautioned that one can never plan the future by the past. Two centuries later, his words are less a caution than an imperative. Each of these five transformations requires reexamination of virtually every social, political, and economic assumption that has directed our past, including those about leadership, what it is, and how it works. Each, taken alone, suggests that traditional top-down, authoritarian models of leadership will no longer work. In combination, they portend that continuation of old approaches will be disastrous.

TRANSFORMATION THROUGH TECHNOLOGY

If we look only at the explosion in technology, the accelerated rate of change has made it such that highly structured, top-down organizations lack the ability to see opportunities in time, react quickly, and stay abreast of critical new developments. Vaill's metaphor of rafting in permanent white water is apt, and when only one or two key people are charged with watching the rapids, there will be unexpected collisions and regular capsizing. Unlike the rafting trips many of us have enjoyed, this one has no guide. No one has run this river before, so the person at the tiller may be no better equipped to chart the course and keep us afloat than are those crouching in the front, watching for the best path through mountainous rapids, or those straddling the sides, pushing us away as the current sweeps us toward the rocks.

A study issued near the end of the last century by the executive search firm Korn/Ferry International predicted that the autocratic, controlling leader—what the study called the "controllasaurus"—would be extinct within a decade. Based on a review of 160 international corporations with in-depth interviews with 75 senior executives, the study forecasts that within 10 years, 60 percent of the firms would be led by teams, and that 85 percent would have some form of decentralized management.[2] In a review of the study in *Nation's Business*, Sharon Nelton attributed this need for leadership change to "shorter product life cycles, intensified competition, and corporate globalization, making the present style of leadership—centered at the top of a hierarchical pyramid—increasingly counter-productive." In Nelton's article, Mary Dingee Fillmore, a Vermont-based organizational consultant, described the new leadership as "less and less seen as something that you do to employees in a kind of autocratic way or for them in a benevolent-despot kind of way. It's really more something you do with people."[3]

Whether those in the academy are willing to admit, the same changes are transforming our colleges. As the nature of work changes, the nature of *preparing* people for work changes, shortening our "product life cycle." A new accountant without complete familiarity with the latest accounting software and with the realities of global competition is unprepared, and an elementary teacher who does not feel at home connecting and guiding students through the infinite world of web resources will not be able to effectively teach.

An editorial written several years later in the trade magazine, *Framing and Forming*, begins: "So the kid you just hired fresh out of engineering school can do second-order differential equations, but can't read a blueprint. Welcome to the club." The editorial reports on results of a survey of its members conducted by the Society of Manufacturing Engineers, focusing on what it calls "competency gaps" among newly hired engineering graduates. The editor admits that engineering schools probably are doing as well as they have ever done, but observes:

> How well would those of us who graduated from engineering schools in the fifties and sixties have been rated by our then-new bosses? Probably not too highly. Not that that's a good reason for being poorly prepared to earn a living as an engineer today, but I wonder how open to change colleges and universities really are? Given that most college instructors are either graduate students, or professors or professor-wannabes who have been confined behind the walls of academia, protected from real-world engineering needs, does it surprise you that today's new graduates still lack the knowledge of what's required of them in industry?[4]

Universities must constantly be scanning the technological waters, anticipating and recognizing significant new currents, and quickly adapting curricula. This will continue to be a weakness until the basic ingredients of participative, team-based, power-with leadership become the norm. The unparalleled changes wrought by technology in the world of information place even greater demands on higher education and its leadership. In an essay in *The Leader of the Future*, California management consultant Judith Bardwick speaks of "the borderless world" and "the borderless economy."[5] Unless we recognize the revolutionary role technology can play in enhancing and expanding access to higher education, we will find ourselves sitting on the sidelines, watching a game that we barely recognize being played by the dozens of entrepreneurial for-profit institutions hungry for that market.

Yet we have not even begun state and national discussions about the effects of these new educational opportunities on traditional academic schedules, transfer issues, financial aid eligibility, split enrollments, and our archaic attendance and residence requirements. The new leadership will have to delicately guide institutions through these mine fields, constantly soliciting the views of students and faculty alike, helping each see opportunities and make decisions with the needs and points of view of all clearly in mind.

Granted, a certain number of students and their parents will still value Division 1 NCAA status as more important than academic excellence, and for a number of decades into the future, there may still be a "Big Something" conference where mega-universities battle on the gridiron for national championship status. Most students, aware that the day they leave the academy they step onto a field where competition is in international board rooms, in global financial markets, and in production of innovative ideas, will opt for the flexible, involving, integrating institution that is fully committed to preparing them for this ever-changing marketplace. Opportunity will be based upon knowledge and the ability to constantly be acquiring it.

TRANSFORMATION AND THE INFORMATION EXPLOSION

The information revolution provides two additional challenges to faculty and to those who lead them. Even the best informed specialist is being forced to again become a learner—of new information concerning the discipline, of new presentation techniques, of new ways to communicate with colleagues and acquire information. A teacher of American History, whom I consider to be among the best I have known, commented recently that he had never been so busy. "I'm having to spend as much time learning as teaching," he said, adding wryly, "and I thought history would remain pretty much the same."

Even with constant immersion in learning, no one is capable anymore of mastering the wealth of knowledge now available—even within very specialized disciplines. Teaching must become an art of facilitation—of teaching students *how* to learn, where to find information, and how to analyze it critically and use it with discrimination. The academic leader will be called upon to facilitate colleague learning and collaboration, just as the professor facilitates it among students.

GEOPOLITICAL TRANSFORMATION

As we in the United States sprint into the twenty-first century, we seem generally aware as a society of the potential effects of the technological and information revolutions—but are oblivious to the probability that we will not leave this century as the world's dominant economy. It has simply not crossed the minds of most Americans that, within a few decades, we could be a second tier economy, stripped of our twentieth-century manufacturing base by inexpensive labor abroad, and of our dominance in innovation and technological supremacy by a failure to advance our own citizens through our education system. The majority of the graduate students in the sciences and engineering are international, many of whom have chosen to remain in the United States after completing their studies to work for American companies. But with both educational and economic opportunity developing in India, China, and the rest of Asia at breakneck speed, it will be much more difficult to attract these students initially and to keep them in our workforce beyond graduation. Europe, Australia, and Canada—all more outward-looking politically and culturally, are emerging as brokers of services to these growing economies, with the United States finding itself in the position of also-ran.

I spent a day touring in China with an account executive of one of America's top information systems corporations—one that has traditionally been identified with the best in innovation, entrepreneurship, and national "image." During the lengthy coach ride between stops, the subject of job outsourcing came up.

"We don't even think in terms of outsourcing," he said. "Outsourcing suggests that there is a 'home' nation for the company, and that we are sending work 'somewhere else.' Our company is a multinational, and we don't outsource anymore. We simply place work around the globe where we can get the best return on our investment in human capital. And we hire people to manage that work who are best suited to function internationally."

If we are to serve as academic leaders in higher education in the new century, we must aggressively improve our national position as a source of valuable human capital. We will probably never compete again as a source of inexpensive labor, so our only recourse is to produce intellectual capital that is globally adept. We have no choice but to forge stronger alliances with our elementary and secondary systems, strengthen and focus curricula in the sciences, mathematics, and language, and insist on performance before we credential a graduate. To do otherwise is to fail to serve.

ECOLOGICAL TRANSFORMATION

The fourth area of transformation during this century need only brief mention. If we are to serve effectively as educational leaders, we must promote and energize the national discussion about how to conserve our natural resources and protect our environment. No student should be allowed to graduate from our institutions without fully understanding the implications of the personal decisions he or she makes on environmental matters. As politically charged as this debate is, it must be held—loudly and continuously in the academy and within the public forums we can influence.

SOCIAL TRANSFORMATION

Peter Senge presents a most thoughtful and cogent discussion about the effects of all of this change on the need for new leadership—a discussion that touches on several of the transformational themes listed above. In his essay, "Robert Greenleaf's Legacy: A New Foundation for Twenty-first Century Institutions," Senge observes that, with the relative international stability of the post–Cold War era, and with our improved mechanisms for stabilizing economies, moderating international disputes, and controlling the other dramatic shifts in our environment which have "created crises" in the past, the nature of crisis has changed. Today's most serious challenges are less tangible, less concrete. They are harder to understand, more difficult to get our arms around, and more slippery to hold onto once grasped.

He attributes this to his observation that new crises are of gradual progression; problems such as poverty, ignorance, racism, and violence. They are problems that have always existed, but which now emerge in the new global, information rich society as less tolerable. They are also internal, and therefore potentially more destructive than crises that we have successfully kept offshore. Yet we refuse to grapple with them, looking instead for more manageable crises; conflicts that we believe have more apparent and manageable solutions.

The most pernicious crises of the new century will not be of the limited war variety that often seems to create distractions from our domestic ills. They will result from the technological and information revolutions just discussed and what these developments will do to the gap in wealth and knowledge that is expanding exponentially. They will be the resultant crises of social dislocation and marginalization—violence, drug use, and ignorance. And one—a contributor to each of the others—will be created by the inability of a hugely bureaucratic education system, both at the primary/secondary and postsecondary levels, to meet the challenge of preparing citizens with the intellectual and social skills, the personal values and sense of responsibility needed to deal with these other challenges.

Virtually all of the four areas of transformation mentioned above will be exacerbated by the fifth; a swelling demand for greater equity and opportunity in a society that no longer legitimizes reasons for limiting or discriminating, but has not found mechanisms for correcting them. Essentially, this transformation is a rejection of top-down, authoritarian models in general, particularly those that have been reflections of the white male as heir to leadership. Women and minorities are no longer willing to tolerate prejudice or discrimination wherever it appears, and this heightened desire for fairness and inclusion now permeates every corner of our society, leading employees to feel more empowered, more entitled to have something to say about how their work can and should affect organizational success.

With years of experience directing the management and leadership programs at MIT (Massachusetts Institute of Technology), surrounded by some of the country's top scientific minds, it is not surprising that Peter Senge is inclined to see emerging relationships between leadership theory and the natural sciences. He also finds in these relationships indications of where the answers to some of the questions raised by these significant societal transformations lie. He notes that, as his colleagues in the physical sciences delve deeper into the world of particle physics, they find that the individual units of energy or matter become less important and interesting in and of themselves. What give them value and usefulness are the forces and relationships that bring and hold them together. Using an expression coined by Buckminster Fuller, Senge refers to this as "patterned integrity." As we deal with the basic, more fundamental crises that will shape our future, it is in the patterned integrity between the human participants, in the force of relationships which brings us together, that we will find solutions, Senge contends.[6] No unit in our society is better positioned to foster this sense of patterned integrity than is higher education, and it becomes one of the new imperatives for leadership service.

There is always a lingering concern that becoming *too* integrated and *too* collaborative in our approach to crisis management and problem solving will stifle the individuality, independence, and unique sense of vision that has characterized us as a nation and as the leading creative force in the world. That is neither the intent nor the result of leadership as service. If properly employed, it invites and celebrates individual creativity and vision. It encourages divergence before convergence, dialogue and debate before decision. It believes in full exercise of Follett's principle of creative crisis, the belief that, if explored honestly and objectively, points of difference and dissonance help focus vision, clarify mission, and channel activity.

> Peter Senge observes in his essay about Greenleaf's work and contribution: Building shared vision is not about people surrendering their individual visions. It is about deepening each person's unique sense of vision and establishing a harmony among the diverse visions so that we can move forward together. It does not require surrendering our uniqueness. If anything, it requires more, not less, of our uniqueness.[7]

What, then, will characterize the educational leader as servant? One of the appeals of the approach is that it does not lend itself to simple lists and formulae. It is leadership of *principle* and of *principles*, not of practices; of *ideas* and *ideals*, not of dogma. There are, therefore, in the ideals of Robert Greenleaf and the principles of Mary Parker Follett, some observations about what the service-centered leader is and does that are worth repeating.

This leader:

- honestly embraces the concept of servant first, showing a willingness to subordinate personal gain to the needs of others;

- shapes a vision of the institution by evaluating its reasons for being and envisioning how those purposes can be accomplished with constant consideration for the welfare and growth of all involved;

- helps others understand and clarify the institution's purposes and encourages them to shape their own vision of how these purposes can be accomplished;

- believes that each person touched by the institution should grow from that experience, coming away from it better able and more inclined to serve;

- believes that each organizational member is a person of value, cares for each person, demonstrates that caring in action and encourages others to do the same;

- is a constant student of the institution and its members, and is continuously listening;

- believes that differences in view are opportunities to clarify vision and direction, and helps institutional members use differences to better understand each other, see the connections between their individual desires, and build common goals, which embrace those interests;

- believes that there are enduring values that include integrity, honesty, trust, and personal responsibility. Demonstrates those values and expects and encourages the same in others;

- accepts the Law of the Situation, believing that each situation contains its solution, but that the best solution will emerge only if as many people as the situation allows are given an opportunity to look for it;

- believes that organizational power is organic, with part of its vitality held by each member. Power is increased and used most fully when it is pooled and exercised as power-with rather than power-over;

- accepts that, if information is power, and power is to be shared, information should be shared as widely as considerations of law and confidentiality permit;

- is open to ideas, willing to risk, quick to praise and slow to judge;

- self-assesses and encourages development of mechanisms for institutional self-assessment. Views bad news as important information;

- carries his or her own burdens, and whenever possible, shares the burdens of others;

- does not ask or expect of others what he or she would not be willing to do, if needed;

- realizes that service within the context of the organization does not mean giving everybody what they want, but means balancing individual desires with the need of the organization to accomplish its mission;

- understands that, to serve as a leader in education, one must have the courage to aggressively present, pursue, provoke, and promote a public agenda that addresses the most important issues of our time and refuse to let the public ignore them.

Where do we find such people? I believe that the world is full of them, and that many are now in leadership roles. All they need is permission and support from those who evaluate the office to begin to transform the institution.

As Octavio Paz stated in the quote that opened this chapter: "The future is a deceitful time and always says to us, 'Not yet,' and thus denies us."[8] But if not yet, when?

In a 1990 interview with Peter Drucker, *Time* magazine reporter Edward Reingold began his interview by asking, "In the remaining years of the 20th century … ," at which point Drucker interrupted and said, "We are already deep in the new century, a century that is fundamentally different from the one we still assume we are in…. For 500 years the new century has always begun at least 25 years earlier."

Reingold asked: "What kind of new century are we in then?"

Drucker's reply was:

> In the 21st century world of dynamic political change, the significant thing is that we are in a post-business society. Business is still important, and greed is as universal as ever; but the values of people are no longer business values, they are professional values. Most people are no longer part of the business society; they are part of the knowledge society. If you go back to when your father was born and mine, knowledge was an ornament, a luxury—and now it is the very center. We worry if the kids don't do as well in math tests as others. No earlier civilization would have dreamed of paying attention to something like this. The greatest changes in our society are going to be in education.[9]

If Drucker was right—that we were already a quarter of the way into the "era" of the new century—and if the changes we need to expect will be in education, we cannot say, "Not yet." Though public perceptions and expectations of education have changed dramatically over the past half-century, the profession's organization and leadership have hardly budged. Continuing to be resistant to change and to new approaches to leadership will not be the death knell for education, just for the "collegasaurus" institutions we have become. Corporate universities will replace us—efficient, flexible, exciting, motivating places where students will be actively engaged in shaping, directing, managing, and evaluating their own learning.

Today's colleges and universities can prevent that revolution through rapid evolution; by becoming those flexible, exciting institutions themselves. But it will require new servant-first leadership; leaders imbued with the ideals of Greenleaf and committed to the principles of Follett. Should we fail to do so, we are likely to find ourselves facing a legislator or former donor who will ask, "Oh, are you people still here? What in the world are you finding to do?"

If we maintain a collective vision based on service to all, then perhaps historians will look back on the beginning of the twenty-first century not as the beginning of the end for the great tradition of excellence in higher education that has marked our past, but as the point of congruence of *six* transformations: in technology, in information, in our geopolitical world, in environmental awareness, in our social order, and in education.

NOTES

1. Alvin Toffler, *The Third Wave* (New York: Bantam, 1980), 10.
2. Sharon Nelton, "Leadership for the New Age," *Nation's Business*, May 1992, 19.
3. Ibid.
4. Art Klein, "Filling the Education Gap," *Forming and Fabricating*, January 1998, 4.
5. Nelton.
6. Peter M. Senge, "Robert Greenleaf's Legacy: A New Foundation for Twenty-first Century Institutions," in *Reflections on Leadership*, ed. Larry C. Spears (New York: John Wiley & Sons, 1995), 224–225.
7. Ibid., 226.
8. Octavio Paz, *Posdata*. Quoted in John Bartlett, *Familiar Quotations: Being an Attempt to Trace to Their Sources Passages and Phrases in Common Use*, ed. Justin Kaplan (Boston: Little Brown and Company, 1992), 736.
9. Edward Reingold and Peter Drucker, "Facing the 'Totally New and Dynamic,'" *Time*, 22 January 1990, 6.

BIBLIOGRAPHY

Allerton, Haidee. "New Numbers." *Training & Development* 50 (1996): 8.

Alverno College. *1996–98 Bulletin*. Milwaukee, WI: Alverno College, 1996.

Ashe, Geoffrey. *Gandhi*. New York: Stein and Day, 1968.

Baum, Sandy. "Approaching the Dilemma from Both Sides." In *Course Corrections: Experts Offer Solutions to the College Cost Crisis*, ed. Robert C. Dickeson, 82–91. Indianapolis, IN: Lumina Foundation, 2005.

Bennis, Warren. *Why Leaders Can't Lead*. San Francisco: Jossey-Bass, 1989.

Bennis, Warren, and Burt Nanus. *Leaders*. New York: Harper & Row, 1985.

Bentley, Arthur F. *The Process of Government*. Chicago: University of Chicago Press, 1908.

The Bible. New Revised Standard Version.

Blumenstyk, Goldie. "Utah's Governor Enjoys Role as a Leading Proponent of Distance Learning." *Chronicle of Higher Education*, 6 February 1998, A23.

Bolman, Lee G., and Terrence E. Deal. *Reframing Organizations: Artistry, Choice and Leadership*. 3rd ed. San Francisco: Jossey-Bass, 2003.

Boyt, Arthur. Personal communication with Kent Farnsworth regarding experiences as a youth, and development of solar racers.

Brown, Lester R. *Plan B 2.0: Rescuing a Planet Under Stress and a Civilization in Trouble*. New York: W. W. Norton & Company, 2006.

Bullard, Charles. "Rawlings: Reject Greed and Begin Era of Giving." *Des Moines Register*, 22 August 1990, A1.

Burns, James MacGregor. *Leadership*. New York: Harper & Row, 1978.

Cable, Carole. Cartoon. *Chronicle of Higher Education*, 16 January 1998, B13.

Callan, Patrick M. "A Ten-year Perspective: Higher Education Stalled Despite High School Improvements." *Measuring Up 2004*. National Center for Public Policy and Higher Education, 2005.

Camus, Albert. *Resistance, Rebellion and Death*. Trans. Justin O'Brien. New York: Alfred A. Knopf, 1961.

Carver, John. *Boards That Make a Difference: A New Design for Leadership in Nonprofit and Public Organizations*. San Francisco: Jossey-Bass, 2006.

"Chronicle Survey of Public Opinion on Higher Education." *Chronicle of High Education*, 7 May 2004, A12–13.

Cleary, Thomas, trans. *Dhammapada: The Sayings of the Buddha*. New York: Bantam Books, 1995.

Cohen, Arthur M and Florence Brawer. *The American Community College*, 4th ed. San Francisco: Jossey-Bass, 2003.

"College Graduation Rates Steady Despite Increase In Enrollment." *ACT Newsroom*, 15 November 2002, http://www.act.org/news/releases/2002/11–15–02.html.

Collins, Jim. *Good to Great*. New York: HarperCollins, 2001.

Collins, James C. and Jerry Porras. *Built to Last: Successful Habits of Visionary Companies*. New York: HarperBusiness, 1994.

"Community College Instructors Demand Higher Wages and Better Benefits." *Chronicle of Higher Education*, 20 March 1998, A10.

Compton, Ronald E. "Re-educating the Corporation." *Corporate Board*, March-April 1993, 1, 5.

Conger, Jay A., ed. *Spirit at Work*. San Francisco: Jossey-Bass, 1994.

Copa, George H., and William Ammentorp. "A New Vision for the Two-Year Institution of Higher Education." *New Designs for the Two-Year Institution of Higher Education*, Executive Summary Report from the National Council for Research in Vocational Education (Fall 1997), http://newdesigns.oregonstate.edu/updates/MDS-1109/section02.html (accessed March 20, 2005).

Covey, Stephen R. *Principle-Centered Leadership*. New York: Simon & Schuster, 1990.

————. *The 7 Habits of Highly Effective People: Powerful Lessons in Personal Change*. New York: Free Press, 2004.

Daggett, Willard R. "Academic and Technical Skills for the 21st Century." Speech, 11th Annual Building Bridges Conference, Missouri Department of Elementary and Secondary Education, Lake of the Ozarks, MO, 16 November 2004.

————. "Technology 2008: Preparing Our Students for Our Changing World," www.leadered.com/pdf/Technology%20White%20paper.pdf (accessed September 17, 2006).

Dawood, N. J., trans. *The Koran*. London: Penguin, 1956.

Drucker, Peter F. "Introduction." In *Mary Parker Follett: Prophet of Management*, ed. Pauline Graham, 8. Boston: Harvard Business School Press, 1996.

————. "Forward." In *On Becoming a Servant Leader*, eds. Don M. Frick and Larry Spears, xi–xii. San Francisco: Jossey-Bass, 1996.

Fisher, James L. *Power of the Presidency*. New York: Macmillan, 1984.

Follett, Mary Parker. *Dynamic Administration: The Collected Papers of Mary Parker Follett*. Eds. Elliot M. Fox and L. Urwick. London: Pitman, 1973.

————. *Freedom and Co-ordination: Lectures in Business Organization by Mary Parker Follett*. Ed. L. Urwick. London: Management Publications Trust, Ltd., 1949.

————. *Mary Parker Follett: Prophet of Management*. Ed. Pauline Graham. Boston: Harvard Business School Press, 1996.

Friedman, Thomas. *The World Is Flat: A Brief History of the Twenty-first Century*. New York: Farrar, Straus and Giroux, 2005.

Gibb, Jack R. *Trust*. Los Angeles: Guild of Tutors Press, 1978.

Greenberg, Milton. "The Power of Academic Citizenship." *Chronicle of Higher Education*, 3 February 2006, B20.

Greene, Jay P. "High School Graduation Rates in the United States." *Civic Report*. Manhattan Institute for Policy Research, April 2002, http://www.manhattan-institute.org/html/cr_baeo.htm (accessed March 20, 2005).

Greenleaf, Robert K. *On Becoming a Servant Leader*. Eds. Don M. Frick and Larry Spears. San Francisco: Jossey-Bass, 1996.

————. *The Institution as Servant*. Indianapolis, IN: Robert K. Greenleaf Center, 1972.

————. *The Power of Servant Leadership*. Ed. Larry C. Spears. San Francisco: Berrett-Koehler, 1998.

————. *Seeker and Servant: Reflections on Religious Leadership*. Eds. Anne T. Fraker and Larry C. Spears. San Francisco: Jossey-Bass, 1996.

————. *The Servant as Leader*. Indianapolis, IN: Robert K. Greenleaf Center, 1991.

————. *The Servant-Leader Within: A Transformative Path*. Eds. Hamilton Beazley, Julie Beggs, and Larry C. Spears. New York: Paulist Press, 2003.

Healy, Patrick. "Arizona Considers Landmark Plan to Allow Community Colleges to Offer Baccalaureate Degrees." *Chronicle of Higher Education*, 16 January 1998, A30.

Helgesen, Sally. "The Female Advantage." In *To Lead or Not to Lead*. Jackson, MS: Phi Theta Kappa, 1995, 1.35–1.39.

Hersey, Paul, and Kenneth H. Blanchard. *Management of Organizational Behavior*. Englewood Cliffs, NJ: Prentice-Hall, 1972.

Hesburgh, Theodore. "Reflections on Voluntarism in America." Vol. XLVI, no. 16. *Vital Speeches of the Day*. Phoenix, AZ: McMurry, 1980.

Hesselbein, Francis "Journey to Transformation," *Leader to Leader* 7 (1998): 6.

Inge, Dean. *The Things That Remain*. New York: HarperCollins, 1958.

June, Audrey Williams. "College Classifications Get an Overhaul." *Chronicle of Higher Education*, 3 March 2006, A25.

Jackson, Phil. *Sacred Hoops*. New York: Hyperion, 1996.

Kaiser, Henry J., Quotation, http://en.thinkexist.com/quotation/i_make_progress_by_having_people_around_me_who/264169.html (accessed September 25, 2006).

Kennedy, Robert F. "Day of Affirmation." *Historical Resources*. http://www.jfklibrary.org/Historical+Resources/Archives/Reference+Desk/Speeches/RFK/Day+of+Affirmation+Address+News+Release.htm (accessed June 15, 2006).

Kidder, Rushworth M. *How Good People Make Tough Choice: Resolving the Dilemmas of Ethical Living*. New York: Fireside, 1996.

————. *Shared Values in a Troubled World: Conversations with Men and Women of Conscience*. San Francisco: Jossey-Bass, 1994.

Kiechel, Walter III. "The Leader as Servant." In *Reflections on Leadership*, ed. Larry C. Spears, 123–124. New York: John Wiley & Sons, 1995.

Klein, Art. "Filling the Education Gap." *Forming and Fabricating*, January 1998, 4.

Kolp, Alan and Peter Rea. *Leading with Integrity: Character-Based Leadership*. Cincinnati, OH: Atomic Dog Publishing, 2006.

Kuhn, Thomas. *The Structure of Scientific Revolutions*. Chicago: University of Chicago Press, 1970.

Lao Tzu. *The Way of Life*. Trans. Witter Bynner. New York: Putnam, 1972.

Lear, Robert. "Rah, rah for new Corporate U." *Chief Executive*, April 1997, 18.

Leatherman, Courtney. "How Some Presidents Keep Their Cool Amid Campus Crises and 60-Hour Weeks." *Chronicle of Higher Education*, 6 February 1998, A36.

Lenzner, Robert and S. Johnson. "Seeing Things as They Really Are." *Forbes*, 159, 1997, 122–128, http://proquest.umi.com/pqdweb?index = 48&did = 11131941&Srch-Mode = 3&sid = 2&Fmt = 3&VInst = PROD&VType = PQD&RQT = 309&VName = PQD&TS = 1150812178&clientId=45249&aid=1 (accessed November 7, 2005).

Levine, Arthur. "Worlds Apart: Disconnects Between Students and Their Colleges." In *Declining by Degrees*, eds. Richard H. Hersh and John Merrow, 155–167. New York: Palgrave Macmillan, 2005.

Lucas, Christopher J. *American Higher Education: A History*. New York: St. Martin's Press, 1994.

Mallard, Kina. "Management by Walking Around and the Department Chair." *The Department Chair*, 10 (1999), quoting W. Edwards Deming, https://secure.aidcvt.com/ank/ProdDetails.asp?ID=DCHAIRSUB (accessed June 13, 2006).

Maxwell, John C. *The 21 Indispensable Qualities of a Leader: Becoming the Person Others Will Want To Follow*. Nashville, TN: Thomas Nelson, 1999.

McGregor, Douglas. *The Professional Manager*. New York: McGraw-Hill, 1967.

McLuhan, Marshall. *The Global Village: Transformations in World Life and Media in the Twenty-first Century*. Oxford, England: Oxford University Press, 1989.

Merrow, John. "Commentaries." *Declining by Degrees*. DVD. Produced by Learning Matters, Inc. Public Broadcasting Service, 2005.

Moorhead, Gregory, and Ricky W. Griffith. *Organizational Behavior: Managing People and Organizations*. Boston: Houghton Mifflin, 1995.

Morrow, Lance. "I Cherish a Certain Hope." *Time*, 3 August 1992, 46.

National Center for Higher Education Management Systems. *College Going Rates of High School Graduates – Directly from H.S.* NCHEMS Information Center for State Higher Education Policymaking and Analysis, 2002, http://www.higheredinfo. org/dbrowser/index.php?submeasure = 63&year = 2002&level = nation&mode =data&state=0.

National Center for Educational Statistics. *Enrollment in Title IV institutions, by degree-granting status, level and control of institution, attendance status, gender, and race/ethnicity: United States, Fall 2002*, http://nces.ed.gov/das/library/tables_listings/show_nedrc. asp?rt=p&tableID=1570.

National Center for Educational Statistics. *Total enrollment in Title IV eligible postsecondary institutions, by degree-granting status, control, and level of institution: 50 states and the District of Columbia, fall 1997*, http://nces.ed.gov/quicktables/Detail. asp?Key=318.

National Geographic Education Foundation. "National Geographic—Roper 2002 Global Geographic Literacy Survey." November 2002, http://www.nationalgeographic. com/geosurvey/download/RoperSurvey.pdf.

Nelton, Sharon. "Leadership for the New Age," *Nation's Business*, May 1992, 18–22.

Newman, Frank, Lara Couturier, and Jamie Scurry. "Higher Education Isn't Meeting the Public's Needs." *Chronicle of Higher Education*, 15 October 2004, B6–B8.

Novak, Philip. *The World's Wisdom*. San Francisco: HarperCollins, 1994.

Oldenburg, Don. "Spirituality at Work." *Washington Post*, 15 April 1997, D5.

Paz, Octavio. *Posdata*. Quoted in John Bartlett. *Familiar Quotations: Being an Attempt to Trace to Their Sources Passages and Phrases in Common Use*, ed. Justin Kaplan. Boston: Little Brown and Company, 1992.

Reingold, Jennifer. "Corporate America Goes to School." *Business Week*, 20 October 1997, 66–72.

Reingold, Edward, and Peter Drucker. "Facing the 'Totally New and Dynamic'." *Time*, 22 January 1990, 6–7.

Richter, Mischa, and Harald Bakken. Cartoon. *Chronicle of Higher Education*, 9 January 1998, B11.

————. Cartoon. *Chronicle of Higher Education*, 16 January 1998, B3.

Rudolph, Frederick. *The American College and University: A History*. Athens: University of Georgia Press, 1990.

Ryan, Kathleen D., and Daniel K. Oestreich. *Driving Fear Out of the Workplace: Creating the High-Trust, High-Performance Organization*. San Francisco: Jossey-Bass, 1998.

Scott, Katherine Tyler. "Leadership and Spirituality: A Quest for Reconciliation." In *Spirit at Work*, ed. Jay A. Conger, 63–99. San Francisco: Jossey-Bass, 1994.

Senge, Peter M. "Robert Greenleaf's Legacy: A New Foundation for Twenty-first Century Institutions." In *Reflections on Leadership*, ed. Larry C. Spears, 217–240. New York: John Wiley & Sons, 1995.

Shahn, Ben. *The Shape of Content*. Cambridge, MA: Harvard University Press, 1972.

Sims, Bennett J. *Servanthood: Leadership for the Third Millennium*. Cambridge, England: Cowley Publications, 1997.

Spears, Larry C. ed. *Insights on Leadership*. New York: John Wiley & Sons, 1998.

————. *Reflections of Leadership*. New York: John Wiley & Sons, 1995.

Spears, Larry C., and Michele Lawrence, eds. *Focus on Leadership: Servant-Leadership for the 21st Century*. New York: John Wiley & Sons, 2002.

Sperber, Murray. "How Undergraduate Education Became College Lite—and a Personal Apology." In *Declining by Degrees*, eds. Richard H. Hersh and John Merrow, 131–143. New York: Palgrave Macmillan, 2005.

Tatum, James B. Personal communication with Kent Farnsworth regarding Servant Leadership, values and spirituality.

Toffler, Alvin. *The Third Wave*. New York: Bantam, 1980.

Truman State University. "Chapter II: History of Assessment at Truman State University," *Truman State University Master Plan* (Kirksville, MO) 1997–2007/May 30th version, p. II-1, http://www.truman.edu/userfiles/academics/masterplan.pdf.

Truman State University Web site. http://www.truman.edu/pages/199.asp.

Vaill, Peter. *Learning as a Way of Being*. San Francisco: Jossey-Bass, 1996.

————. "A Fireside Chat with Peter Vaill." *Peter Vaill Presentation*. Indianapolis, IN: Robert K. Greenleaf Center for Servant-Leadership, 1996. Recording.

Walker, Pamela. "A Case Study on Servant-Leadership" (EdD diss., University of San Francisco, School of Education, 1997).

Wheeler, David L. "More Students Study Abroad, but Their Stays Are Shorter." *Chronicle of Higher Education*, 17 November 2000, A74.

White, E. B. *Letters of E. B. White*. Ed. Dorothy Lobrano Guth. New York: Harper & Row, 1989.

Whitman, Walt. *Walt Whitman: Complete Poetry and Selected Prose and Letters*. Ed. Emory Holloway. London: Nonesuch Press, 1967.

Williamson, Marianne. *A Return to Love*. New York: HarperCollins, 1992.

Woolman, John. *The Journal of John Woolman*. Ed. Janet Whitney. Kila, MT: Kessinger, 2006.

INDEX

About the Author

KENT A. FARNSWORTH is Mary Ann Lee Endowed Professor for Community College Leadership in the College of Education, The University of Missouri – St. Louis, where he directs the Center for International Community College Education and Leadership. He is President Emeritus of Crowder College, Neosho, Missouri, where he served for 19 years.